CARLYLE MARNEY:

A PILGRIM'S PROGRESS

Carlyle Marney
1916-1978

CARLYLE MARNEY:

A PILGRIM'S PROGRESS

by
John J. Carey

With a Foreword by
Samuel S. Hill, Jr.

Mercer University Press
Macon, Ga. 31207

Carlyle Marney: A Pilgrim's Progress

From *Faith in Conflict* by Carlyle Marney. Copyright © 1957 by Abingdon Press. Used by permission.

From *The Coming Faith* by Carlyle Marney. Copyright © 1970 by Abingdon Press. Used by permission.

From *He Became Like Us* by Carlyle Marney. Copyright © 1964 by Abingdon Press. Used by permission.

From *Recovery of the Person* by Carlyle Marney. Copyright © 1963 by Abingdon Press. Used by permission.

From *Structures of Prejudice* by Carlyle Marney. Copyright © 1961 by Abingdon Press. Used by permission.

Quotations from *Priests To Each Other* are reprinted with permission of the Judson Press, Valley Forge, Pennsylvania.

Quotations from Marney's unpublished sermons, lectures and notes are published with the permission of Mrs. Elizabeth Marney and the Marney Literary Estate.

Second Printing.

ISBN   0-86554-001-2

Copyright © 1980 by the Mercer University Press, Macon, Georgia 31207.

Library of Congress Catalog Number: 80-82573
Printed in the United States of America

To

Mary Charlotte McCall

—who shares Marney's roots in the South,

his hopes for its future,

and

who is one of his "New Breed."

PREFACE

This study was made possible by a research grant from The Center for the State of Southern Culture and Religion at Florida State University. The Center is interested primarily in movements, issues, and persons influencing the contemporary South, and I am grateful to the Advisory Board of the Center for their support of this project. The grant freed me to spend much of my time in 1979 researching and writing; it also enabled me to travel to North Carolina where I had access to Marney's unpublished papers. I am especially indebted to my colleague Richard L. Rubenstein, Director of the Center, whose continued endeavors have been instrumental in the Center's funding and research programs; to the Rockefeller Foundation and the Merrill Trust, who have given the Center the bulk of its support, and to Karen Bickley, the capable Research Associate of the Center, who facilitated my work in many ways.

Mrs. Elizabeth Marney welcomed me to the Marney home at Wolf Pen Mountain and graciously allowed me to work with Marney's unpublished papers and files in his study for an extended period in June of 1979. She was an invaluable source of information as I sought a better understanding of his life, personality, and their common venture for 38 years. Marney's sister, Evelyn M. Phillips, currently Associate Professor of Church Music Education at Southwestern Baptist Theological Seminary in Fort Worth, Texas, shared with me memories and materials relating to life in the Marney home in Harriman, Tennessee. She also alerted me to the Marney tapes which are available in the library of Southwestern Baptist Theological Seminary. Marney's daughters Susan and Chris shared memories and impressions of their father and helped me to understand him within the context of family life. Marney's life-long friends, Theron Price and L.D. Johnson, both of Furman University, shared their recollections as Marney's fellow students at Southern Baptist Theological Seminary in the early 1940's. Marney's aunt Faye Marney of Knoxville reminisced about her special nephew and sent me a packet of family clippings about his life and achievements. James A. Berry, Marney's Minister of Music at both Austin and Myers Park, wrote me about his first contacts with Marney in Paducah and sent me copies of their early correspondence. Erna Alsdurf of Lake Junaluska talked with me at length about her work with Marney at Myers Park and at the Interpreter's House. Mary Kratt of Myers Park Baptist Church in Charlotte sent me a copy of the booklet she edited for the Church, entitled *Marney*; the booklet brings together reminiscences of 50 people of that congregation about Marney's days at Myers Park, and is an excellent source for insights into Marney's personality and style. Other persons too numerous to be listed here shared with me their encounters and memories of Marney, and to all I extend my thanks.

Harriet Leonard of the Duke Divinity School Library sent me copies of Marney's out-of-print books, and other resources were sent promptly by the staff of the Emory University Library. The library staff at King's College, London, helped me locate materials on English thinkers upon whom Marney drew. Thomas A. Langford of the Duke Divinity School and Samuel S. Hill, Jr., of the University of Florida both made helpful suggestions to me as I initially shared with them my interest in making this study. James A. Fowler of Emory University, Literary Executor of the Marney Estate, was helpful and encouraging on many fronts. My colleague Walter L. Moore, Jr., read the book in manuscript form and made a number of suggestions for clarification and emphasis. Jan DeCosmo and Karen Bickley of the Center for the Study of Southern Culture and Religion collaborated on the typing of the manuscript. Nancy Myers-Blumberg, secretary *par excellence* of the Department of Religion at Florida State, assisted me in countless ways at all stages of my research and writing, and handled all of my requests with efficiency and dispatch even when they came amid an already overcrowded professional schedule. My debts to all of these friends are reminders of how much of scholarly work is held together by invisible threads of assistance and encouragement.

Mary Charlotte McCall brought her writing talents and skills as a former Law Review Editor to bear on the first draft of this manuscript; in addition, she assumed a disproportionate share of responsibility for our home and children while the book was being written. Men joined with me in the experience of being married to a feminist will appreciate the value of those gifts. Our children Joanna and Jessica frequently interrupted my writing with questions about "Mr. Marney" and came to speak of him as though he were a member of our family. They especially liked his funny stories, and I learned to kneel to their eye level when recounting them.

I did not know Marney well personally, but I lived within his orbit when I took my first professional position in Salisbury, North Carolina from 1957-60, and when I was at Duke from 1963-65. I met him at Union Theological Seminary in New York in 1961 and, like many throughout the South, heard Marney stories for over twenty years. Prior to embarking on this study, I knew his theological writing but had not studied it systematically. In language that Marney's friends will recognize — the trip has been worthwhile. This task has been far more than an academic exercise. I am especially pleased that Sam Hill, who shared life's pilgrimage intimately with Marney and whose work has done so much to explain the spirit of Southern religion to the broader nation, agreed to write a Foreword to the book; he also read the book in manuscript form and made a number of suggestions for precision and clarity.

Two stylistic features of the book need clarification. Since this book will be read by some who only knew Carlyle Marney by reputation, it should be pointed out that for most of his adult life he was known simply as "Marney." Other than for a few references to him as a boy, I have consistently used that appellation for him. Secondly, in his writings and sermons Marney always tended to use masculine terminology when referring to the individual, the believer, and the totality of humanity (e.g., "our proper manhood"). I have occasionally modified his reference to include men and women, but there is a limit as to how much modification one can do without distorting Marney's own vocabulary. Where I do exposition of Marney's thought, I have left his use of masculine terminology intact, but I have done so mindful that most people today would prefer the use of more inclusive language.

It is appropriate for me to express my pleasure that this book is published by the Mercer University Press. Marney spoke on the

Mercer campus many times and had numerous friends on the faculty. The director of the Press, Watson E. Mills, took an early interest in this manuscript and guided its path to publication with more than professional competence.

I mined a rich vein, and the wealth of the raw materials was invigorating. The power of Marney's thought and vision was bound inextricably with the force of his personality and the thrust of his humor. I have tried to capture all three in this portrait. To the extent I have succeeded, it is a testimony to the quality of the subject. The flaws, unfortunately, are my own.

John J. Carey
The Florida State University
Tallahassee, Florida

TABLE OF CONTENTS

FOREWORD

My profoundest personal recollections of Carlyle Marney can all be summed up in the assertion, Golly, he could make you feel good. Marney was alive. He strode into a room or your company or onto a podium and everything vibrated. He engaged everybody and everything in his orbit. Power flowed through him with incredible force.

Foreword writers are permitted—nay, more, expected—to speak personally. Never mind, in this case I could do no other. When Marney came to my father's church in Louisville to make a talk, I, being the pastor's twelve-year-old son who had already been spied as a future minister, was asked to introduce him. "Golly, he could make you feel good." When I had yielded the floor to the main speaker—you weren't sure who that was during his response to the introduction — he turned the spotlight on me. His encouraging words sustained me for days. He knew how to ingratiate without flattering you.

During the years of my father's presidency at Georgetown College, we ranked Marney first among the many celebrities who stayed in our home. He was different, refreshing, entertaining, colorful. He was engaging; he took us seriously, each and all. Looking back, I have to wonder at my father's great attraction to him. I judge that it was little more than Marney's blending of down-home warmth, humor, and dazzling capacity with words and ideas. That may seem enough, yet the differences between those two men were sufficient to have short-circuited the genuine friendship they developed. I guess it is also a tribute to Daddy that he was responsive to big people of less traditionalist persuasion in whose league he was marginally equipped to travel by both experience and native ability. But, back to Marney, he brought out the best in a great many people.

Who could not take notice or ever forget the encouragement given by a distinguished man to a younger colleague in his professional life? Well, I couldn't. He was manifestly grateful for my being his daughter's teacher. So much so that he once remarked that I (a professor at Chapel Hill) might be the only man in North Carolina of whom he was jealous. On other occasions, he wrote so approvingly of my published work and would say aloud, "Sam, we're proud of you." The last two times we were together, we embraced spontaneously in a Duke office and quaffed a pitcher after an evening's ecumenical session in Memphis where, more than a little irritated by the propositionalist minds present, he needed to talk. Strangely, he didn't like my departure from Baptist ranks to join the Episcopal Church, but if we had talked about it—how I wish we had—he would have urged me on still further in the pilgrim's progress which he had helped me see to be the cadence of the Christian life.

John Carey's book takes us deeply into the personality and mind of the man with whom I had these kinds of experience. He was an outstanding person, I want to say, a "compleat human being." The closest correspondence linked his Christian Humanism with the manner and character of the man himself. At least these characteristics deserve to be accented: his capacity for growth; his intellectual brilliance; his unbelievable skills with people; a perceptiveness about issues and people which was matched by courage and compassion; a magnificent sense of humor; gifts for speaking and conversing—few people have both—which place him in the first echelon of the top-flight leaders I have known; an impatience with conservative religion which, having heated up, could wither its proponents.

If human beings are identifiable by what things we are patient with and what things we are impatient with, Marney can be aptly characterized as a Christian of classical to liberal leanings poised on the waves of modern developments in a historical process he believed to be guided by the eternal God for the making whole of all people. He had no time for suspicions about modernity, for fixated interpretations of truth, for any hint of honoring Truth over Persons or even ranking them in relation to each other. He could be quite caustic toward biblical or theological propositionalists. Yet the stories are legion of his reaction to his own fulminations. Commonly he sought out the persons whose point of view he had just devastated for a reassuring and reconciling conversation. I remember so vividly that after that Memphis dialogue he summoned me to a corner to ask whether I thought he had been too hard on the Evangelicals present. Honesty demands the recognition that Marney too had his problems with correlating Truth and Persons. He had a theory of language and substance which addressed the problem successfully, but emotionally his response was awkward not infrequently (the frequency increasing as he got older.) "Compleat human being" means sinner as well as saint, having hang-ups as well as grace-traits, failure to follow through with your own convictions. Marney's people, the Southern Baptists, had taught him about sinfulness very effectively, his own just like that of all others.

In the chapters that follow John Carey tackles the formidable task of penetrating Marney's relation to his setting: the South and the Baptist tradition in it. We learn much from him about that enigma. Maybe it will be useful for someone else to try his hand—a tough job it is—from somewhat different perspectives. I want to begin with the contention that Marney was an "intellectual mutation." Simply no one and nothing in his own circumstances can account for the twists and turns his career took. He was Carlyle Marney, period. Nor is this an uncommon phenomenon; surely a notable proportion of great people arrive at destinations for which background and environment have not directly prepared them. Marney was simply an exceptionally gifted person, a man who possessed certain kinds of genius.

But we want to be able to say more than that, and we can. Carey insightfully applies Tillich's category of "on the boundary" to Marney's thought. I believe that category can also be applied to his social setting, the time and place of his earthly pilgrimage. It was his lot to stand between southern generations, between the "New South" and the much-less-southern South. He was reared in the "New South," a context which sought "progress" but within the traditional value-world of retaining the region's culture as the framework of meaning. Prevalent judgments and dominant leaders alike were simply assumed to be of that region; alien points of view and people, when they did intrude, were weighed and found wanting, mostly for little better reason than that they were different. But Marney attained cultural majority during and after the years of World War II, a watershed in southern American history. This historical accident put him astride a boundary since the world in which he hammered out his professional career and adult life was increasingly more national (and global) and less provincial. John Carey traces this pilgrim's progress from traditionalism to new awareness and concerns, and finally to a Christian Humanism which bore the marks of his headlong encounter with secularized modernity.

The die was cast for the overturning of the South's rigid racial structure by the social consequences of that great War. The lethargy and reactionism of the 1950's could do no more than delay the destruction of the old racial structure; indeed 1954 occurred during those 1950's! Then all hell broke loose late in that decade and throughout the next. The South has been "much-less-southern" from that time forward.

This superficial treatment acquires validity only when we realize that southern religious leaders (and other kinds) were far from free to transcend their environment before 1950 or so. The evidence suggests that "liberated" Southerners were few and far between from the Reconstruction and Jim Crow eras until then. Not that the numbers of such dissidents grew much after the Second War, however. What really changed lay in the realm of attitude. Before that turning point, those who "broke free" usually manifested one or the other of the following reactions: (1) A tortured mind and conscience. Efforts to depart from convention or to change denominations (double meanings intended) were characterized by struggle. It was ever so difficult to just change or just leave. You had dues to pay, gratitude to give, explanation to offer. (Marney himself was fond of advising young proteges to "bless their origins.") And not only couldn't you quite pull yourself away, they wouldn't let you leave. Snipping the religious and cultural (mainly the latter) umbilical cord just wasn't approvable behavior. They didn't want you; they also couldn't conceive of your leaving, for where else was there to go? (I can't forget the response of a good friend to the news that I would soon be delivering a sermon in a Lutheran church. She wanted to know what I would be preaching about.) (2) A complete, clean break. Most of those who exchanged their heritage for a wider world just left. They registered no public rejection of the nurturing institutions, fought no battles, suffered through no heresy trials—they just left. What is significant about this development is that those who embodied it moved cleanly into a different sphere. *They* were *not* boundary people. Whatever their reasons and resources may have been, they were able (mostly at least) to disengage themselves from their past. Their vocational and personal lives were practiced by the affirmation of a different way without decisive reference to the old which had been outgrown.

Marney belonged to the boundary generation of southern religious personalities. Neither the tortured struggle nor the clean break characterized his career-long "tilting" with the denomination which gave him birth and education. One can hardly abstain from playing amateur psychiatrist to speculate that he was saved from either course by the sheer force of his personality and brilliance. Many a human being who might predictably have crumbled or retreated from following his gleam has been prevented from doing so because he "had so much going for him" (or she. .her, of course). One suspects that his exceptional strength had much to do with Marney's being his own man. But it is also likely that conditions were becoming more opportune for an independent spirit in the 1940's than even a decade earlier, most certainly than during the South's supremely provincial era in the half-century after Jim Crow. Marney happened along in the first years of the transition period. He was one of the last from the marginal generation. He may have been the first Southern Baptist minister to have continuous interchange with people from other denominations and regions of nation and world, who at the same time could decide to stay in the South and not bolt from the denomination. Before him, you couldn't leave—even if you left; since the 1960's leaving has been an increasingly less wrenching experience.

As a person of comparable background and orientation who reached maturity a decade later than Marney (and is more mortality prone), I can attest to the anguish of enlarging your world. But the reasons have less and less to do with a tortured conscience or the application of pressure by family, friends, and denomination. Now unfamiliarity with alternative options, as to philosophy and institution, is the chief force creating barriers against movement by a good many who aspire to considering it. It is astonishing how many enlightened people there are who, craving dialogue toward growth, do not know where to turn to seek it. All of your references and referees belong to your same circle; they are institutional colleagues. (As we shall see, that fact is complicated, being also bound up with one's personal attitudes and temperament.) Of course such a condition is partly attributable to the absence of ecumenical connections in

Southern Baptist life. Marney deplored that state of affairs at least from 1946-1948 when he served his first congregation following seminary years; his founding Interpreter's House twenty years later was an extension of the same concern. I confess that I harbor a strongly negative attitude toward my own Southern Baptist people (whom I can never altogether leave) at one (and only one) point, the same as Marney's: they never told me about the "world-wide Church of God" (Marney's term).

Why have the Southern Baptists been so provincial and uncooperative? They have not only stood apart, they have also not been able to wish you well and "keep fellowship" with you as you moved. Here is a massive company of souls, fully at home in their society, indeed dominant in it, hardly retiring or beleaguered, and a people much involved in civilization through the sponsoring of innumerable eleemosynary and educational agencies. How can a body so much in touch with the world have confined its viewpoints and restricted its people to such a narrow angle of vision? Let me propose three answers as hypotheses (which I hope someone will test) for explaining this puzzling phenomenon.

The first we may call the momentum of history. The Southern Baptist Convention may come fairly close to being the institutional continuation of a very old southern identity with its peculiar regional values and styles. Some wag's claim that when the Confederate States of America died, the Southern Baptist Convention arose to take its place is largely but not altogether facetious. If you find yourself a part of that community, it is far easier to ride along with it than to challenge it or seek alternatives to it, particularly in view of its enormous success, the huge circles of friends and programs it provides you, and its nice cultural fit.

The second is precisely its ethnicity. If you belong in it, you readily tune to its rhetoric, its signals, its nuances of thought, humor, logic, lore, music, bodily posture, and all the rest. Outside it, you are thrown off your stride. Southern Baptist people do not participate easily or well in programs or discussions carried on through the communication systems of other organizations. They are regularly on a different wavelength. They often feel inferior. Incidentally, this is as characteristic of their dealings with Evangelicals as with the mainline denominations. The Southern Baptists haven't been much more conspicuous in national Evangelical circles than among mainline ecumenical Christians. These of course would not be major problems for a people accustomed to hearing alternative sounds. They are not, a fact due in part to the vast formative influence they have wielded on southern Christianity generally. Beyond those factors, the communication system with which they are familiar is but one dimension in a cultural network where religion and much more are intimately interconnected. I refer, obviously, to the culture of the southern region.

The third answer to the riddle, why are the Southern Baptists so aloof from fellowship and cooperative endeavors with other Christians, is theological. Theirs is a compressed theological understanding, boiling down to a theology of Atonement. All roads lead to and from the cross, at some cost to Creation, Resurrection, Incarnation, nurture, and churchmanship. They are preoccupied with the theme of Redemption. Most sermons, much understanding, nearly all witnessing concentrate on the meaning of Christ's death. Many strengths do attend this clear vision. Nevertheless it suffers from the lack of richess and depth in the formulation of what Christianity means and what the Christian community undertakes. For our purposes here this item has significance in that the scope of understanding, being greatly restricted, does not facilitate enjoyable interchange of ideas or deeds with other Christians who acknowledge many facets (or who live by some other preoccupation). In a nutshell, their cultural complacency is joined by inexperience with other (more inclusive) visions of the Christian faith and the responsibilities of churchmanship. It is true that they feel a little estranged from other Christians and somewhat inferior to them; it is also the case that they do not need or enjoy different company. They are a unique breed of people, holding together in curious ways some sectarian and some other cosmopolitan qualities. They are not to be mistaken for Fundamentalists or radical sectarians.

Carlyle Marney was far from alone in taking exception to the curiosities of that paradoxical condition; or, in being able to deal with it, absorb it, or overcome it, variously. Long before him John A. Broadus and E. Y. Mullins of the mother seminary in Louisville managed. His older contemporary Harold W. Tribble did it with some success, as did Wayne E. Oates from his own generation. His younger contemporary John R. Claypool is doing it with an ease which bespeaks more than his personal healthfulness; he came along later than the boundary time, the marginal generation, the rise of the much-less-southern South. Parenthetically, Claypool gave the 1979 Lyman Beecher Lectures at the Yale Divinity School; Marney had been invited to give those lectures in 1980. There are thus exceptions to the rule that the Southern Baptists go it strictly alone. In truth, however, nearly all of them have had academic rather than pastoral appointments, and the total of all such is incredibly small within a thirteen million member denomination.

In passing, we should note that a much larger group of scholars reared in the denomination has moved on to stature and prominence in the wider academic world, the majority of them having affiliated with another denomination. Prominent examples are Liston Pope of Yale; Davie Napier of Yale, Stanford, and the Pacific School of Religion; Walter Harrelson of Chicago and Vanderbilt; John Maguire of Wesleyan and the State University of New York; James Crenshaw of Vanderbilt; and Dan Via of the University of Virginia. Some who now enjoy national reputations are remaining Southern Baptists in denominational institutions; for example, Charles Talbert of Wake Forest, Edgar McKnight of Furman, and Joseph Callaway of the Southern Baptist Theological Seminary— all of these, significantly, in the area of biblical studies. Even that company has precedents, however, such as E. Y. Mullins himself, and A. T. Robertson, a Southern Seminary scholar in New Testament studies who attained to international renown in the 1920's.

Notwithstanding his tensions with the Southern Baptist Convention, Marney's thought was transparent to a number of qualities he shared with his Baptist people and doubtless learned from them. One was his exalting religious experience over doctrinal requirements. A second was his capacity for being down-to-earth, for relating to people warmly. A third was his magnification of the place of preaching. A fourth was his belief in growth, that the Christian life consists of going "wherever the Lord leads." A fifth was his deep dedication to religious liberty. Neither he nor the denomination scored a perfect mark on these five items, but all ranked as strong commitments for both.

I happen to know that the brand new Mercer University Press had competition in securing the contract for this book. It is fitting and— from Marney's perspective which is also my own—deeply heartening that Mercer won out; this means that a Southern Baptist institution is bringing this study of a "major heretic" to the public. Mercer University has a long tradition of commitment to academic freedom, a quality closely related to religious freedom which is a much treasured Baptist value. Its Christianity Department has been in touch with the larger world at least as far back as the membership on its faculty of the distinguished church historian Albert H. Newman early in this century. Today it comprises Baptists trained both inside and beyond the Southern Convention and of one member from another fellowship within the Baptist communion. The author of this book is an ordained minister of the United Church of Christ and, worse than that, a Hoosier. The composer of this Foreword has been treated with uncommon graciousness for he is a *former* Southern Baptist. (Some of his friends insist that he is a "Southern Baptist Episcopalian.") The passion for Christian liberty and brotherhood for which Carlyle Marney strove so mightily is thus mirrored in the circumstances of this endeavor toward bringing his life and thought to light.

He was a giant of a man. His ministry was vast in quantity and of incalculable quality. He bailed out hundreds who were in distress. How much he meant to so many of us southern boys starving for food, straining for light, and grasping for courage! And, Golly, he could make you feel good. This Baptist-Episcopal mutation must conclude by offering a prayer that Marney's great God may grant our beloved brother an eternal pilgrim's progress now that "the gates of larger life" have been opened to him.

Samuel S. Hill, Jr.

CHAPTER I

INTRODUCTION: WHAT MANNER OF MAN IS THIS?

The man who stands on many boundaries experiences the unrest, insecurity, and inner limitations in existence in many forms. He knows the impossibility of attaining serenity, security, and perfection. This holds true in life as well as in thought.

—Paul Tillich, *On The Boundary* (New York: Charles Scribner's Sons, 1966), pp. 97-8.

Southern Religion and the Baptists

The Southeastern United States has long been recognized as the most conventionally religious section of the country. It has produced regionally prominent preachers and been a fertile territory for the evangelists of several persuasions, but with rare exception it has not brought forth religious leaders of national stature in the twentieth century. Distinguished scholars at Southern universities and divinity schools have been in the front ranks in Biblical studies, theology, and ethics, but on the whole these scholars have addressed academic audiences and have not been native Southerners. Interpreters of national religious currents and sensitivities do not find many indigenous white Southerners among the ranks of those who have shaped the twentieth century American mind. In his important volume *Southern Churches in Crisis*, Samuel S. Hill, Jr., pointed out that the national image of Southern religion has been predominantly shaped by the "Baptist-Methodist Syndrome," which stresses revivalism, the conversion experience, and personal ethics set in a political ethos favoring states' rights, white supremacy, laissez-faire economics, and property rights. Although Hill did not take the Black churches into account in his otherwise definitive study, he illumined the "Southern Style" of church life and uncovered the roots of Southern religious parochialism. Since his work was published in 1966, the South and Southern religion have become topics of special interest for scholars and lay people alike. Although new writers have pointed to recent and modest changes in the Southern religious climate, most interpreters agree that Hill's insights about Southern religious regionalism remain valid.

The extensive scope and influence of the Southern Baptist Convention have been a major force in Southern white religious insularity. Although outsiders often assert that the Convention is more "Southern" than Baptist, it is nonetheless the largest Protestant denomination in America, claiming 12,917,922 members, 35,031 churches and 55,300 ordained ministers.[1] Those who know the denomination will recognize its internal diversities, but looked at within the American theological and ecclesiastical spectrum it has been a major conservative force. Certain churches (*e.g.*, Watts Street Baptist in Durham, University Baptist in Austin, University Baptist in Chapel Hill, Pullen Memorial in Raleigh, Myers Park in Charlotte, University Baptist in Winston-Salem) have histories of progressive leadership and engagement with pressing social questions, but they are isolated islands in a large sea of fundamentalism. Similarly, Southern Baptist colleges, universities, and seminaries have existed in varying degrees of tension with the more parochial and literalistic elements of the tradition. Vigorous within its own social and cultural context, the Southern Baptist Convention casts an enormous shadow over the entire South and remains a troubling enigma to mainstream Protestantism, with ecumenical charity often strained by Baptist militancy.[2] The Southern Baptist Convention affirms believer's

---

[1]See Constant H. Jacquet, ed., *1978 Yearbook of American and Canadian Churches* (New York and Nashville: Abingdon Press, 1978). *ad. loc.*

[2]It is beyond the scope of this study to consider the characteristics and diversity of the Southern Baptist Convention (SBC) in greater detail. Representative works which

baptism and the gathered church, champions a conservative approach to scripture (often manifested in assertions of biblical inerrancy), and has consistently refused to join the ecumenical bodies such as State Councils of Churches, the National Council of Churches, or the World Council of Churches. Its regionalism, separatism, and conservatism — undiluted by the varying class structures found within its ranks — are hallmarks on the American religious scene.

Marney: What Kind of Baptist?

Against this background of Southern regionalism and Baptist separatism, the life and career of Carlyle Marney (1916-1978) are particularly interesting. Born and raised a Baptist in East Tennessee, he attended a Baptist College and a Baptist Seminary. He became a nationally prominent preacher and theologian while serving Baptist churches in Austin and Charlotte. Distinctively southern in his roots, speech, and mannerisms, Marney nonetheless broke the stereotypic Baptist mold. Articulate, socially conscious, and ecumenical, he served on task forces of the National Council of Churches and the World Council of Churches. He sat on the editorial boards of the leading ecumenical journals *Theology Today* and *Religion in Life* and was a trustee of *The Christian Century*. He preached in leading university and college chapels across the country and worked easily with men and women of all faiths as he undertook assignments for the Chaplain's Board of the U.S. Army. He moved freely in prestigious

---

illumine the history, theology, and social attitudes of the SBC include O. K. Armstrong and Marjorie M. Armstrong, *The Indomitable Baptists: A Narrative of Their Role in Shaping American History* (Garden City, N.Y.: Doubleday and Co., 1967); Bynum Shaw, *Divided We Stand: The Baptists in American Life* (Durham, N.C.: Moore Publishing Co., 1974); John L. Eighmy, *Churches in Cultural Captivity: A History of the Social Attitudes of Southern Baptists* (Knoxville: University of Tennessee Press, 1972); George D. Kelsey, *Social Ethics Among Southern Baptists, 1917-1969* (Metuchen, N.J.: Scarecrow Press, 1973). Many cultural contrasts between the SBC and the broader Baptist tradition are pointed out in Winthrop S. Hudson, *Baptist Concepts of the Church* (Valley Forge, Pa.: Judson Press, 1959) and James E. Tull, *Shapers of Baptist Thought* (Valley Forge Pa. :Judson Press, 1972). Southern Baptist influence on white Protestantism in the South is considered in Kenneth K. Bailey, *Southern White Protestantism in the Twentieth Century* (New York: Harper and Row, 1964). Recent articles exploring distinctive facets of the Southern Baptist Convention include C. Penrose St. Amant, "Southern Baptists and Southern Culture," *Review and Expositor,* Vol. 67 (Spring, 1970), pp. 141-52; James T. Baker, "Southern Baptists in the Seventies," *The Christian Century,* Vol. 90 (June 27, 1973), pp. 699-703 and his "Scalping the Ephraimites: Southern Baptists in the '80's," *The Christian Century,* Vol. 97, No. 8 (March 5, 1980), pp. 234-257.

academic circles and taught at Austin Presbyterian Theological Seminary, the Duke Divinity School, Virginia Military Academy, and the summer sessions of Princeton Theological Seminary. He wrote insightful and well-received theological books (mostly published by a Methodist press) and in 1976 was awarded the University of Glasgow's highly esteemed D.D. Degree. He smoked a pipe, drank bourbon, and expressed himself in the vernacular. Many a national audience heard him and asked, "What kind of Baptist is this?" Some of his confreres in the ministry asked the same question, as did more than a few of his parishioners.

Marney was a rare Baptist and a rare churchman. Although he knew and loved the Baptist tradition, he spent most of his professional career tilting with its theological and ecclesiastical structures. On most issues of denominational policy, he went against the stream. While in Austin and Charlotte (1948-67), he became a symbol for young Southern Baptist ministers and seminarians that the tradition could be lived in another way. The twentieth century is indebted to several distinguished Baptist thinkers (Walter Rauschenbusch, Harry Emerson Fosdick, Martin Luther King), but Marney is by general consensus the only white Southern Baptist preacher-theologian to attain national ecumenical stature. It is appropriate, therefore, that his life and thought now be evaluated for a broader audience.

Problems of Perspective and Method

It is not an easy task, however, to put Marney's thought into a systematic perspective. For one thing, he was not a systematic thinker. He made no effort to bring his writings together into a coherent whole. He met no classes in systematic theology. His books, usually thematic in structure, were often shifting considerations of a common motif. He wrote for pastors and lay people, not for academicians or theologians. His books are filled with illustrations from literature, history, and personal experiences. He moves from narrative to recollection to "stream of consciousness" writing with little concern for demarcation. This is understandable when one realizes that most of Marney's writings were originally designed for the ear, but it does not make his writing easy to follow, nor does it facilitate a comprehensive grasp of his thought.

In addition, Marney's thought was expressed in diverse ways. Beyond his published books and articles, one must take account of unpublished sermons, tapes (some available in cassettes and others on file in such places as Duke University, Southwestern Baptist Theological Seminary in Fort Worth, Texas and Union Theological Seminary in Richmond, Virginia), rough outlines in his files, and even a distinct "oral tradition" which grew up around him. (The oral tradition is so extensive that it practically made Marney a legend in his own lifetime.) Any interpreter of Marney faces the task of assimilating, distilling, and harmonizing these various materials. There is considerable repetition within his tapes and lectures—not surprising for one who addressed so many diverse audiences—but consistent themes reappear. It is my judgment that up to 1970, the most important of Marney's ideas found their way into print, although some themes were developed more extensively in informal addresses. After 1970, however, many ideas were developed in papers prepared for discussion at the Interpreter's House, and others found their most lucid expression in sermons. This study draws on all these sources, including at times the oral tradition.

Finally, Marney never compiled a bibliography of his published articles and sermons, nor did he keep any systematic files of his sermons or lectures. Working through his files and unpublished papers was a formidable task. Many of his writings, particularly in the last decade of his life, circulated to friends and colleagues in mimeographed form, and he sought no other publication of them. His support staff was too small and the demands of his professional schedule too great for him to catalogue, correlate, or cross-reference his work. As I poked my way through files and papers, unmarked boxes and stacks of material, Marney's associate Erna Alsdurf told me that Marney was probably chuckling in his grave to think of someone trying to make sense of it all.

Marney was not a static thinker: priorities of one decade gave way to the demands of the next. But that is true of all creative thinkers, and it behooves us to read him with the same openness of mind that he brought to his work. In thought as in life, Marney was a pilgrim, and any study fair to him must convey the sense of the journey.

Despite these complexities, careful reflection on Marney's life and thought reveals a *cantus firmus* upon which he based most of his understanding of Christianity, the nature of the church, the task of theology, and the goal of the ministry. The term *cantus firmus,* taken from Bonhoeffer, describes a fundamental melody at the heart of a composition. It is an appropriate metaphor for one so fond as Marney of musical imagery. To be sure, even the *cantus firmus* alters in the thirty years from 1948 to 1978, but this study attempts to uncover a theological substratum beneath the wide diversity of topics which drew Marney's attention. Those who heard Marney only occasionally or read only one or two of his books will find here a perspective which clarifies Marney's basic convictions. For those more familiar with the wide range of his thought, I hope this volume will illumine the sources of his thought, place him within the theological context of his times, and clarify his significance for Protestant theology.

Marney frequently referred to himself as a "viator," a traveler; one on the move, a perpetual sojourner; one who knows not, but believes; who has not, but hopes for; who sees not, but obeys. The pilgrim motif provides the methodological clue for this study and explains its title. The book is oriented to Marney's pilgrimage both in life and in thought, and considers Marney in evolutionary perspective. Each of the following chapters approaches the task from a different angle of vision. Chapter II examines Marney's life and notes the personal and professional transitions reflected in his career. His mountain background, his gifts with language, his interests in history, his skills as a story teller, and his candor were all part of his effectiveness with Texas cowboys and Ivy League students alike. The life pilgrimage sets the context for his related intellectual journey. Chapters III and IV deal with Marney's thought, paying particular attention to his changing perspectives and priorities. Chapter III considers Marney's theological stance during his days as pastor in Austin and Charlotte, a period spanning nearly twenty years, and analyzes the intellectual influences on him during that time. Chapter IV concentrates on the developments of Marney's thought in the last decade of his life (1967-78) while he was Director of the Interpreter's House at Lake Junaluska, N.C. Both his audience and his interests shifted in that period, and the chapter illumines Marney's search for new categories in his effort to reach those outside the Christian tradition. The Conclusion attempts to tie together the man and the message and offers a perspective on Marney's significance as pastor and theologian.

Marney as Boundary Person

There is value in understanding Marney as "boundary" person. His was the forthrightness of the mountaineer tempered by keen perception and the subtleties of southern wit. He lived out his life crossing the boundaries between rural and urban life, between civilian and military life, between Southern Baptists and the broader Church in America and the world, between Christianity and Humanism, between the Church and the University, and between security and change. To live and think on the boundary, as Tillich once aptly noted, is never an easy task, for it subjects one always to misunderstanding and criticism. It seems clear, however, that Marney relished the creative edge which life on the boundary provides.

This study is neither a definitive biography of Marney nor exhaustive of the themes and subtleties of his work. More time and perspective would be required for those achievements. I hope, however, that this book will enable readers to understand and better appreciate one of the South's creative thinkers—one who combined the art of ministry, the talent of proclamation, and the gift of writing about as well as any Christian leader of his generation. To know Marney is to know the South dealing forthrightly with issues of life · and faith in the twentieth century.

So now we ask: who was this man, and what was his pilgrimage?

CHAPTER II

MARNEY THE MAN:
REFLECTIONS ON A PILGRIMAGE

"Of Schopenhauer it was said, 'He is not a philosopher like the rest; he is a philosopher who has seen the world."

—W. MacNeile Dixon, *The Human Situation*
(London: Edward Arnold and Co., 1937), p. 15.

The Roots in East Tennessee (1916-1940)

In the early 20th century, Harriman, Tennessee, nestled into the Cumberland mountains about forty miles west of Knoxville, had a population of some 3,500 people. Earlier immigration patterns had resulted in a sizable number of northerners settling in the area, and Harriman was more cosmopolitan than one might expect of a small mountain town. The region stood with the Union at the time of the Civil War and thus never developed the intense Confederate mentality characteristic of countless other small southern towns. Harriman rested on an economic base of agriculture and jobs provided by the W.J. Oliver Foundry, which produced plows and other farming implements. Coal mining, timber production, and iron works were likewise a part of the life and economy of Roane County.

Leonard Carlyle Marney was born into that world on July 18, 1916. His father, John Leonard Marney, unschooled beyond the fourth grade, came to Harriman from an outlying farm at the age of 16 to work for the W.J. Oliver Company. He eventually became a designer of turn plows, and was an active Baptist layman who pioneered a mission program for indigent people of Harriman. Marney's mother, born Sarah Victoria Mays, had been left an orphan and lived for a number of years with her grandfather. She eventually came to Harriman and lived with a northern family which owned mills in the city. Marney's sister Evelyn described their mother as "ambitious" and their father as "steady and hard working." Both were active in church affairs; Marney later recalled how his mother would regularly attend both the Baptist and Methodist Churches of Harriman to be sure that she was "all right." Both parents were determined mountain folk who believed that all persons should reach their highest potential.[1] Neither of them was sympathetic to the old Southern tradition of slavery, nor were they in favor of segregation. Mrs. Marney loved music, and instilled that love in all her children.

Leonard and Sarah Marney had three children, of whom Carlyle was the eldest. Their daughter Evelyn was deeply influenced by her mother's musical interests and eventually pursued a career in church music. The youngest child, Milton, became interested in physics and philosophy and combined those interests as a scientist and policy planner at George Washington University. Carlyle is remembered by his sister and aunts as having been an active, fun-loving boy, interested in the out-of-doors, mischievous on occasion, but always polite to older people. He was in the Boy Scouts, played the trombone (in the style of Homer Rodeheaver, whom his parents admired), sang solos with the high school chorus, and won three varsity letters in football. Long before entering the ministry he is remembered as having a gift for speaking and persuading others to his point of view. Although a bit uneven in his academic performance, he was recognized by a number of teachers as a gifted child and was encouraged to pursue his academic interests.

At home Carlyle shared in many tasks, including the family garden, made trips with his father, and discovered the world outside of

---

[1]This information, and other pertinent information about the Marney family, was obtained from Mrs. Phillips in an interview and written recollections sent to the author.

Harriman by reading. His mother, long persuaded of the value of education, encouraged him to develop the habit of regular reading. Marney said on several occasions that during his boyhood he must have read over three thousand books from the Andrew Carnegie Library in Harriman.

Unlike many mountain towns, the industrial base and mixture of northern and southern families in Harriman provided a variety of cultural resources. There were the Chautauqua Lecture Series (for which Marney's mother regularly saved ticket money), lectures from prominent politicians (such as Elihu Root and various United States Senators), Shakespearean touring companies, bands, and symphonies. Remembering Harriman in those days, Marney observed:

> Within an eight block area of this little town of 3,500 souls...I can now recall the graduates of Harvard College...Yale University, University of Tennessee, of Kentucky, of Alabama, of Georgia Tech, the Cincinnati Conservatory, and Cornell. A representative of Canadian culture at its best lived across the street and supervised 12 million acres of forest . . . There were products of Louisville's best society. My neighbor had retired from a distinguished Philadelphia pastorate to serve the Presbyterian (northern) Church. A professor of economics at the University of Tennessee was a pastor of the Christian Church. There was a lot of Yankee commercial connections with timber, coal and iron. There was a revolutionary war heritage, there were some devoted Roman Catholics, two splendid Jewish families, there was Boy's Week and Boy Scouts, photography, music, water sports and all kinds of visiting pretty girls from Chattanooga. All in all, there was in Eastern Tennessee a fantastic pluralism... There was capital from New York (the East Tennessee Land Company has still nearly a half million acres), there were industrial families from the north and midwest...There were remnants of the social experiments of sons of the British royalty who took up 100,000 acres and left behind their little libraries, their Anglican missions and tennis. There were the New England cults (the universalists had a temple of grand proportions a block away) and temperance societies and social projects and Harvard's silent graduate just four doors

away. These all had their weight on us. And mostly it's still there.[2]

One must be cautious, however, about waxing too lyrical about the cultural richness or distinctiveness of Harriman as an East Tennessee mountain town. It existed within a broader ethos of rural political conservatism and Biblical fundamentalism. It was, in fact, only some 40 miles across the hills from Dayton, the scene of the famous Scopes Trial of 1925. Marney later noted that the Scopes Trial was the first news story he could remember and recalled his confusion as a nine-year-old boy to realize that the *Cincinnati Post* and the *Knoxville Sentinel* took different sides on the issues raised by the trial. Marney always remembered the Scopes Trial as a major event of his childhood and as a point of embarrassment for the South. His essay, "Dayton's Long Hot Summer: A Memoir," written many years later, described the trial and set it in theological and cultural perspective. It is, in my judgment, one of the most valuable pieces Marney ever wrote about the South and his childhood.[3]

The political and cultural mindset of the Marney family was solidly conservative. Marney recalled:

In general, we supported William Jennings Bryan against Clarence Darrow at Dayton, Henry Ford, who was paying $5 a day in Detroit - if one could just get there, Congressman J. Will Taylor, the American Legion, the First National Bank, Charles A. Lindbergh, baptism by immersion, the Republican party, the Junior Order of United American Mechanics, the Anglo-Saxon race, the competency of the individual, the Fourth of July parade, Mother's Day, the Volunteer State, the abortive attempt of certain east Tennesseans to kidnap the Kaiser near the close of World War I, and the Tennessee Central Railway...The Knoxville *News Sentinel* was our newspaper, and the Baptist churches furnished our worship and religious education...We talked about Socialists, the Soviet armies, the Zionists, Felix

---

[2]"Dayton's Long Hot Summer: A Memoir," published in Gerry Thompkins, ed., *The Scopes Trial: Forty Years After* (New York: Charles Scribner's Sons, 1965). I was unable to locate a copy of this book but did find Marney's typed copy of his manuscript.

[3]*Ibid.*

Frankfurter, Negroes and Eleanor Roosevelt with various degrees of like or dislike.[4]

Marney's own family diversity created in him an intensive ecumenism. His grandparents were Methodists, as were four aunts and an uncle. One uncle was a Presbyterian, another an Episcopalian, and among other aunts and in-laws there were Catholics and Unitarians. Marney later observed that family Sunday afternoon gatherings were "more or less a debate as to who had it best." He also observed that the Methodists, being in the majority, usually won. The Marney home was next door to the Presbyterian manse, so over the years the Marney family were friends with a series of Presbyterian ministerial families.

All of his life Marney was influenced by his happy boyhood, his warm family life, and the experience of growing up in a secure place. His sermons from his years in Austin and Charlotte were sprinkled abundantly with memories of his experiences as a child: scout trips, swimming in the summers in the Tennessee River, trips with his father, admonitions from his mother, dynamics with his siblings. He was eulogized at his memorial service in Charlotte as one who had never left East Tennessee behind him.

In spite of his reading program at the Carnegie Library and strong emotional support from his family, Marney was not really prepared for the world of college, although Carson-Newman, which he entered in 1933, was hardly a place of broad cultural sophistication. A rather typical Baptist church-related college, it drew predominantly upon young Baptist men and women of East Tennessee. Marney entered college on a football scholarship, and his first two years at Carson-Newman were, in the words of one family member, "academically disastrous." Clearly Marney was more interested in football and social life than in academic pursuits. He was advised by the Dean after his sophomore year to take a leave of absence from the school and to reflect more seriously on the meaning of college education. During his leave of absence Marney worked as a ditch digger and experienced the drudgery of sustained manual labor. For the first time, he appreciated the value of a college education. The summer prior to returning to Carson-Newman, Marney was inspired by an itinerant evangelist and committed himself to a vocation in church work. He returned to Carson-Newman in the fall of 1936 with a new sense of purpose and finished his undergraduate days as a serious student and campus

---

[4]*The Structures of Prejudice* (Nashville: Abingdon Press, 1961), pp. 125-6.

leader. Many years later, Marney recalled being re-baptized in his college church. This was an unusual practice, but Marney felt it was necessary to symbolize a new and genuine dedication, in contrast to the immaturity which he felt characterized his earlier baptism in his home church.

Within a relatively short period of time Marney was asked to become music director of the Training Union at his college church. That invitation drew on his recognized musical skills, both vocal and instrumental. A few months after that, he was asked to be general director of the Training Union. "Barely dry from his baptism" (as Marney humorously recollected), he was apprehensive about undertaking such a major responsibility, but finally agreed to do so because he knew it would be a good experience. The experience was so influential, in fact, that upon his graduation from Carson-Newman in June, 1938, Marney decided that he would become a full-time educational worker in the church. Pursuing that goal, he accepted a summer job directing the educational program at the First Baptist Church in Bristol, Tennessee, and in the fall of 1938 took a position as Educational Director of the First Baptist Church of Kingsport, Tennessee.

The Kingsport days were exciting ones for Marney. He related warmly to the senior pastor, J.G. Hughes, and was especially effective in working with the church's young people. He met an attractive young music teacher from Kingsport, Elizabeth Christopher, who, though a Presbyterian, instinctively liked this outgoing Baptist. A romance blossomed which captivated Marney for the rest of his life. Although Marney enjoyed his work in all facets of the church's educational program, he eventually decided to move from educational work into the fuller range of the parish ministry. The impetus for his decision was an illness of the senior minister, which required that Marney assume preaching responsibilities for several months. Marney had only limited experience in preaching, but he responded well to this opportunity and was warmly received by the congregation. In these months, his wife was later to observe, "a preacher was born." The courtship with Elizabeth flourished, and they were married in June, 1940, at the Kingsport Church. The following fall Marney began his studies for the ministry at Southern Baptist Theological Seminary in Louisville.

Theological Education and The Beginnings of Ministry (1940-1946)

Classmates of Marney's at Southern Baptist Seminary recall that he entered the Seminary like most other students: poor and relatively conservative in outlook. He arrived wearing the culture of East Tennessee. Southern Baptist Seminary was known throughout the denomination for having a tradition of learned and independent-thinking faculty members. The Seminary had its problems with the denomination: Crawford Toy was fired from the faculty in 1871 because of his sympathies for biblical criticism, and President W.H. Whitsitt had been dismissed in 1901 because of a theological dispute. The Seminary mirrored the tension between evangelical faith and serious scholarship, and the student body—uneven because of admission policies which allowed some students to enter without undergraduate degrees—divided according to priorities given to faith or scholarship. The faculty, however, had a number of progressive and courageous spirits, and the shadows of these professors lay across Marney's shoulders for the remainder of his life.

W.O. Carver, Professor of Missions and Comparative Religion, illumined Marney on the diverse streams of the Christian tradition. S.L. Stealey, who eventually became Marney's major professor for his Th. D. dissertation, intrigued Marney with his knowledge of Church history and, in particular, with his interests in the pluralism and diversity of the Church in the first centuries of its life. Hersey Davis, who occupied the Chair of New Testament, was influenced by German biblical scholarship and took an open position towards source criticism and form criticism as methods of study of the New Testament. Harold Tribble, later to become President of Wake Forest University, taught Marney the rudiments of theological method. Professor Theron Price, currently Professor of Religion at Furman University and a seminary classmate of Marney's, recalls that Marney was a voracious reader and was held in awe by his fellow students because of his extensive familiarity with the many volumes of the Ante- and Post-Nicene Fathers. (Price remembers wryly that "Marney was like most other students there, except he was smarter."[5])

Marney was also deeply influenced during his Louisville days by Charles L. Graham, long-time pastor of the Crescent Hill Baptist Church in Louisville. Graham was a bachelor and lived on the campus of Southern Baptist Seminary after his retirement from the Crescent Hill Church. Marney had virtually a father-son relationship with

---

[5]Interview with the author. Other recollections of the Louisville years were provided by Elizabeth Marney and L. D. Johnson of Furman University.

Graham, and in fact wrote most of his doctoral dissertation in Graham's apartment. Graham later visited the Marneys in Austin and left Marney his entire theological library. Marney saw in Graham a man of great statesmanship, integrity and strength. He once said that it was from Graham that he learned all that he knew about the discipline of preaching.

Not unexpectedly, Marney's days at Southern Baptist Seminary were days of theological evolution and growth. Neither his family nor friends can recall any sudden period of enlightenment, but rather remember Marney as a "pilgrim," moving day by day into newer and deeper perspectives on the Christian tradition.He developed perspectives on biblical studies and church history which were to set him against the assumptions of biblical fundamentalists inside and outside the Southern Baptist Convention. Later in his career, Marney observed:

> Fundamentalism is not a rational position or a logical theology, though it has its premises, its rationale and its literal equational format. Fundamentalism is emotive, a bias, a provincialism that new information cannot change. It is a *neurosis.*[6]

While Marney was pursuing his Th.M. degree he agreed to serve a small congregation at Fort Knox, Kentucky. It was his first practical experience as a parish minister and gave him a modest amount of income to help defray school expenses. The little Baptist Church he served was eventually incorporated into the ambit of Fort Knox, but at the time of his service it was on the periphery of the base and served predominantly families of enlisted men. When the small congregation of thirty-one people asked Marney to be their pastor, they said they could only pay him $14 a week for two Sundays preaching a month. Marney, moved by their modest situation, agreed to serve the church under these circumstances and said that in addition he would conduct services on the other two Sundays each month free of charge. The congregation, touched by the good faith and commitment of their young student, called him to be their pastor and never failed to pay him. As a measure of their appreciation for Marney's leadership they subsequently raised his stipend to $17.50 a week.

Fort Knox was the headquarters of the First Armored Division of

---

[6]"Dayton's Long Hot Summer," p. 15.

the U.S. Army, and Marney became increasingly involved in leadership and counseling for base personnel. These were his first contacts with the military world and they helped him to understand the problems of chaplains who were trying to minister to men being trained in the art of warfare. Marney later estimated that in his years at Fort Knox he came to know 10,000 men of the First Armored Division.[7] Race riots in the Fort Knox prison stockades in 1940-41 provided his first exposure to America's bitter social cleavages. His ministry to Fort Knox personnel and their families enabled him to see that career military men (and others who participated in military structures for limited periods of time) still have genuine personal needs. That awareness prompted Marney to apply for an appointment to the chaplaincy, but he was turned down because of his poor eyesight.

Marney subsequently had his quarrels with America's "super-patriots," but he never denigrated the significance of the military for a free society or spoke condescendingly about career military officers. Many of his later sermons were illustrated with experiences of his at Fort Knox and from reports he received from former parishioners who fought World War II and Korean war battles with the First Armored Division. Never a pacifist, Marney felt that both the reality of evil in the world and the need of the nation to defend itself required a well-trained, professional military.

Marney completed his Th.M. studies at Southern Baptist Seminary in 1943. After graduation, he was encouraged by S.L. Stealey to stay on and pursue Th.D. studies. He continued his work at Fort Knox until 1944, and then accepted a call to the First Baptist Church of Beaver Dam, Kentucky. That entailed commuting to and from the Seminary, but the pay was better and a manse was provided. Family expenses were greater, too: a daughter, Chris, was born in 1944. The years of Marney's doctoral program (1943-46) were difficult. The demands of the academic program were heavy, and Marney carried a full range of pastoral responsibilities at Beaver Dam. Elizabeth Marney recalls that they were poor and had difficulty buying furniture for the large manse. Marney eventually completed his dissertation in 1946 on the topic "The Rise of Ecclesiological

---

[7]"Preaching the Gospel, South of God," *The Christian Century,* Oct. 4, 1978, p. 916. This article, published posthumously, is a transcription of an interview conducted with Marney in August, 1976, by Bill Finger of the Southern Oral History Program.

Externalism to 337 A.D." The dissertation was never published, although it is clear from Marney's papers that he had subsequently done some revision of it with a hope of seeing it in print. The dissertation deals with the emergence of church offices and organizational patterns during the first four centuries of the Christian era. The focus of the dissertation explains much of Marney's lifelong interest in early church history, and particularly his familiarity with the work of the great German scholars Adolf von Harnack, Hans Lietzmann, Johannes Weiss, and Reinhold Seeberg. His own Baptist heritage led him to take seriously questions of freedom and authority in the early church, as well as the question of pluralism in its ministry. The dissertation also explains Marney's familiarity with the Ante-Nicene church fathers and his special attraction to Irenaeus.

An interesting bit of Marney oral tradition which lingered around Southern Baptist Seminary was that he was the only student in the history of the Seminary who read all of the Ante-Nicene and Post-Nicene Fathers in the original Greek and Latin. Years later while Marney was visiting the Seminary, a graduate student asked Marney at a reception whether the story was true. Marney reported: "I took him by the arm, led him to an isolated corner where no one could hear us, looked him in the eye and said, 'Son, it's a lie.' "

When Marney received his Th.D., he was thirty years old and had gained considerable experience in preaching and pastoral work. A number of his professors encouraged him to reply to several teaching overtures or at least to settle in a city where he would be close to a college or university. Marney, however, sensed his calling differently and decided to remain in the parish ministry.

Kentucky Poverty: Immanuel Church, Paducah (1946-1948)

Shortly after receiving his degree in 1946, Marney accepted a call to the Immanuel Baptist Church in Paducah, Kentucky, and spent the next two years of his life serving that large, predominantly blue-collar congregation. In the late 1940's Paducah was a city of approximately 34,000 people, strategically located in southwestern Kentucky at the confluence of the Ohio and Tennessee Rivers. The city had regional importance because of its proximity to the Tennessee Valley Authority and the atomic Energy Commission in Oak Ridge. Although the city had a relatively stable economic base because of the surrounding agricultural productivity (corn, tobacco and livestock were the primary commodities), it was also shaped by the impact of Kentucky rural poverty. No responsible minister could serve in the area without grappling with the tragedies of systemic poverty.

Immanuel Church was substantially larger than Marney's previous congregations at Fort Knox and Beaver Dam, and it made greater demands on his professional skills. Fortunately, for the first time Marney could serve as a pastor without the complications of school work, and he threw himself into the preaching and pastoral tasks with all his energy. It was the first time he had a staff of any size to work with, and that by itself led him to experiment with new forms of ministry. Unfortunately there are no extant copies of Marney's sermons preached in Paducah. As he did through most of his ministry, he spoke from notes and not from manuscripts, and the Church did not record his sermons. Marney preached at two Sunday services and also at Wednesday evening prayer meetings. Professionally and theologically Marney differed from many of his Baptist confreres with his critical approach to biblical studies and preaching as well as in his ecumenical spirit. While at Paducah, he began to speak at youth gatherings around Kentucky and Tennessee, and to make occasional appearances on college campuses. As was the pattern among talented, young, and enthusiastic preachers, he conducted revivals and special services at other Baptist churches in the area. This pattern of speaking on campuses, at youth assemblies, and at other churches continued throughout the next thirty years of his ministry.

Marney also formalized the worship services at Immanuel Church. He had the bulletins printed rather than mimeographed. Copies of these services are found in Marney's papers, and they show (for a young Baptist!) a marked interest in liturgy and music. An insistence on high quality musical selection and performance was then -- and continued to be -- a hallmark of Marney's ministry. His sister Evelyn served as Minister of Music while Marney was pastor, and it was a rewarding experience for both of them. It was also at Paducah that Marney met James A. Berry, who was to become his Minister of Music in Austin and Charlotte. Berry was at that time a student at Westminister Choir College in Princeton and had married a woman from Immanuel Church. He would occasionally sing at services when they returned to Paducah. Marney was impressed with him , and that began a relationship which spanned twenty years.

A second daughter, Susan, was born in 1947, and Marney responded warmly to the delights and demands of fatherhood. Elizabeth assumed the primary responsibilites of nurture and child care, but like many fathers of daughters, Marney took a special delight in both Chris and Susan. Fatherhood, however, had to find its way amid the complex professional demands of the ministry.

The levels of poverty in and around Paducah made a lasting impact on Marney, and, like Reinhold Niebuhr before him, Marney was struck with the Church's ineffectiveness in understanding, let alone changing, a social order which incorporates such tragedy and inequity. Although untrained in the social sciences, Marney recognized that traditional statements of faith and piety failed to deal with the economic complexities and class self-interests which are indigenous to systemic poverty. This experience was grist for his mill when from 1967-78 he served on the United States Commission on Rural Poverty. In Paducah, Marney was exposed to the problems of illiteracy, cyclical unemployment, the vicissitudes of the market place, and the deep alienation of rural Kentucky from the mainstreams of American society. Reflecting on his Paducah days, Marney observed: "I learned all I know about poverty, hope, and native dignity in a huge old church in Paducah."[8]

It was also at Paducah that Marney began to sense the ambiguities of the ministry as a profession. As many a young pastor has found out, it is one thing to attempt to serve God with one's life and to struggle to be a preacher of the Word; it is quite a different thing to deal with denominational structures, to recognize that success in the profession requires compromise, and to realize that succumbing to temptations can be masked with lofty theological language. It was at this point, Marney later recalled, that he made three vows concerning his career as a minister, namely: "1) I would never become economically victimized by a job, 2) I would never want anything a denomination could give me to the point of paying too much to get it, and 3) I would follow new light into anyplace as soon as I knew it to be new light."[9]

These convictions stayed with Marney for over thirty years and were guidelines for ministerial integrity. As he thought them through in Paducah, however, he did not realize that new light was soon to dawn which would dramatically change the direction of his life and ministry.

---

[8] "Dayton's Long Hot Summer," p. 14.

[9] "The New Breed's Man" (New York: American Baptist Convention, 1967), p. 5. See also *The Coming Faith* (Nashville: Abingdon Press, 1970), p. 141.

The Coming of Southern Recognition: The Call to Austin (1948-1958)

The public-speaking ability of this young pastor in Paducah soon became a subject of conversation in the broader circles of the Southern Baptist Convention. While attending a meeting of the Southern Baptist Convention at Memphis in 1948, Marney was approached by Dr. Frederick Eby of Austin, Texas, concerning the vacant pastorate at the First Baptist Church of Austin. After preliminary negotiations, Marney accepted a call from Austin. In every way, it was a staggering decision: it entailed a move from his native Tennessee/Kentucky region to the Southwest; from a small town to a capital city (population 160,000) in the largest state in the union; from a blue-collar to a white-collar and upper-middle-class congregation; from a rural ethos to a university city; and from a moderate-sized congregation to a large congregation of 4,000 members with a staff of twenty people. Yet, Elizabeth Marney recalls that young as Marney was at the time (32), he never had any doubt that he could handle this assignment. With two young daughters, a supportive wife, and mountaineer determination, Marney accepted the pastorate of the First Baptist Church of Austin.

The First Baptist Church of Austin was not known as a center of progressive theology or churchmanship prior to Marney's arrival. His predecessor, W. R. White, was a moderate and gracious man, active in Baptist denominational circles, but never controversial in style or forceful on social issues. The Church was best noted for its prestigious membership; it attracted governors, state legislators, supreme court justices, ranking officials of state government, university professors, and an impressive cross-section of the business and professional families of Austin. It had a strategic location opposite the State Capitol and was the largest church in the city. The Church had an annual budget of over $200,000, had around 1,500 active in its church school, supported ten missionaries, and under Marney's leadership began to take more seriously its ministry to the University of Texas, located only one-half mile away.

Marney was exhilarated by Austin and the educational level of his congregation. He built a congenial and supportive staff and developed deep, life-long friendships with fellow ministers Blake Smith of University Baptist Church and Ed Heinsohn of the University Methodist Church. His ecumenical perspectives deepened, and his intellect was honed by his engagement with university-based humanists, philosophers, and skeptics. He met influential people: Sam

Rayburn, Lyndon Johnson, Bill Moyers (as a young man), Brooks Hayes, Price Daniel, leaders of the Texas Legislature and Judiciary, and prominent bankers and business leaders. Reflecting on the Austin experience, Marney observed:

> I fell off into a pit of beautiful influences, minds, and opportunities. I thought I was at the navel of the earth. I was preaching to classic people who could understand my criticisms and my affirmations. Perhaps 15 or 20 people — like Jim McCord, who was then Dean of the Austin Presbyterian Seminary, and Fred Ginascol in the Philosophy Department at the University of Texas, the historian Walter Prescott Webb and pastors Blake Smith and Ed Heinsohn — created the most exciting, stimulating, agonizing, debating, acrimonious, insulting, uplifting hours of discussions — sometimes all night. I also taught at the Presbyterian Seminary. I offered my wares to the Baptists south of God in terms of manuscripts and other things, which they rejected. Without my seeking it, Presbyterian, Methodist, Episcopal, Catholic and secular doors opened.[10]

Just as Marney liked Austin, he liked the wide open spaces of Texas. Its cultural pluralism, western life-style, and capacity for humor all touched facets of Marney's personality. He told his Austin congregation that a Kentucky friend had written him to congratulate him on moving to Austin and to wish him well in his ministry there. The friend went on to observe that he had visited Texas himself, and thought that the only things the state needed were more water and a better grade of people. "I told him," said Marney, "that was also all that hell needs." The congregation responded to Marney, and he quickly felt at home with them.

The outspoken mountaineer eventually came into conflict with more established powers of his congregation over matters of church governance and the role of the minister. At every previous church he served, Marney had been his "own man" and was free to plan worship services and programs consistent with his understanding of the Gospel. He felt that a Board of Deacons, unless it could show persuasive theological reasons for not doing so, should be supportive of a minister's plans to expand the ministry of a Church. Just after Marney had completed one year in Austin, however, his leadership

---

[10]"Preaching the Gospel, South of God," p. 916.

was challenged by a man who had been Chairman of the Board of Deacons for over 25 years, and who had in fact been influential in the Church's extending a call to Marney. For this man — conservative in politics and in theology — Marney was moving too fast, too soon. Marney did not always consult him or obtain his prior approval on new ideas for the Church. Marney was thus seen as a threat to the small cadre of established families who had controlled church policy during the tenure of several of Marney's predecessors. The leader of this group finally sought a meeting with Marney and told him he should resign. Marney, unintimidated, called for a congregational meeting to adjudicate the dispute and was vindicated by a vote of 696-16. The issues in the dispute were as much personal as administrative, but the situation was a paradigm with which many other ministers can identify. Affirmed by the congregation, Marney stayed nine more years, and always spoke appreciatively of his congregational support and freedom of the pulpit in Austin.

During his Austin years, Marney served as Adjunct Professor of Christian Ethics at the Austin Presbyterian Seminary and, was a consultant and supporter of the nationally known Faith and Life Community at the University of Texas. He achieved national prominence with the publication of a volume of sermons, *These Things Remain* (Abingdon, 1953), and his cleverly written volume *Faith in Conflict* (Abingdon, 1957). He discovered that he liked to write, and that his homiletical interests had a larger audience through the printed page. His long-time ties with Abingdon Press began in these early years in Austin. He participated in a weekly television show and a number of his talks were published for broader circulation around the state. He was known for his outspoken opposition to all patterns of racism and segregation years before the epoch-making *Brown v. Board of Education* decision of the U.S. Supreme Court in 1954. He was concerned not only with the plight of blacks but also with the discrimination against Mexican-Americans in so many areas of Texas. He began the process of transforming the image of the First Baptist Church from a traditional church into a more theologically liberal, socially progressive congregation.

It was also during the Austin years that Marney criss-crossed the state of Texas speaking to student assemblies, filled prominent pulpits of other large southern churches, and came to be recognized as one of the outstanding preachers in the Southern Baptist Convention. He knew the world of Baptist discourse, and how to reach audiences of a conservative biblical background. His gift for exegetical preaching enabled him to open such audiences to a deeper understanding of the Christian tradition. It is a tribute to Marney's Austin success that many years later (in January, 1974) he was invited back to be the plenary speaker at a joint meeting of the Texas Council of Churches with the Texas Constitutional Revision Committee.

Just as Marney learned about poverty in Paducah, so in Austin he learned about the tentacles of racism. He had to meet with black friends at an out-of-the-way Mexican restaurant. Working with Blake Smith and Ed Heinsohn, Marney was influential in lobbying against racist bills introduced in the Texas legislature. On one particularly tense occasion, with thirteen blatantly discriminatory bills pending on the floor of the legislature, Marney invited Congressman Brooks Hayes of Arkansas to come to Austin to speak against such legislation; he also prevailed upon Price Daniel, then governor of Texas and a close personal friend, to introduce Hayes. Hayes spoke at a rally held at the First Baptist Church, and all thirteen bills were killed in the legislature.

Marney preached regularly at First Baptist Church and frequently twice on Sundays. Wednesday evening services were held, and Marney did his share of those as well. He spoke from outlines, but the sermons were taped and subsequently transcribed. While doing reasearch in Marney's library, I came across the unedited transcriptions of Marney's sermons during his Austin years. I will comment on the theology of those sermons at a later time; suffice it to say here that the sermons reflect a wide familiarity with the Bible, and in style are reminiscent of Fosdick's approach to "life situation preaching."

Marney combined theological acumen with a sharp instinct for human dilemmas, and had a gift for dressing sophisticated insights in illustrative garb familiar to his hearers. Two small books of Marney's from this period grew out of sermons about family life and show how he combined life situation analysis with biblical insight. *Mothers and Sons* (Austin: The Cumberland Foundation, 1954) treated the mysteries of mothers and sons in an evolutionary manner, showing how what is communicated at all stages of that relationship eventually colors all male styles and attitudes about females. *Dangerous Fathers, Problem Mothers and Terrible Teens* (Abingdon, 1958) depicted many of the stereotypes which are so destructive to family communication and pleaded for more understanding of others by all parties concerned. The volume contained some theology, some psychological and sociological insights, and a lot of common sense. Neither of these volumes is weighty by today's theological or social science standards, but they are good testimonies to Marney's posture as a pastor-theologian in his Austin years.

Recognition also came from other professional directions. Through his contacts with the military established during his Fort Knox pastorate, Marney continued to receive invitations to speak at army posts, air force bases, and various naval schools. Particularly memorable to Marney was his invitation to serve as a "missioner" for the Army and Air Force in Korea and Japan during September, October, and November of 1954. It was his first (and only) exposure to the cultures and religious traditions of the Far East. He was forced to look at Christianity as a religion deeply shaped by western culture, yet in his diary of his trip he observed that he could not see in any of the eastern religions a serious alternative to the spiritual power of Christianity. He was struck, however, by the cultural differences of East and West, and was deeply moved by the loneliness of the servicemen to whom he was speaking. The trip made a lasting impression.[11]

Other civic and professional responsibilities came to him as well. Various denominations sought him out for their assemblies. The Texas Council of Churches had him address plenary sessions. Teaching at the Presbyterian Seminary opened doors into that tradition. He spoke at national scout jamborees, to assembled cowboys on big ranches, to businessmen in Dallas-Fort Worth, on state-wide television programs, and on governmental occasions. He turned down a constant stream of invitations to take academic posts in colleges, universities, and seminaries, and declined frequent overtures from other churches. He felt that the First Baptist Church of Austin had the potential to influence the State of Texas and the southwest, and he wanted to facilitate that mission. The mountain man thrived in the rugged southwest.

It is worth noting that Marney's talents were utilized more widely in other denominations and civic areas than in the Southern Baptist Convention. Although he had a network of close friends scattered in prominent Baptist churches throughout the south, Marney was regarded in Baptist administrative circles as a "renegade" and was not allowed into high councils of the denomination. Those who knew

---

[11]Marney's diary of the trip remains unpublished, but is available among his private papers.

Marney well into his Austin years recall his irritation that the Southern Baptist Convention did not join the National Council of Churches, his disappointment that the Texas Baptist Convention would not take an open stand on the race issue, his dismay over much of the educational material produced by the Southern Baptist Convention, and his continual skirmishing with fundamentalist pastors who resented his style, popularity, and theology. In his sermons and talks, Marney proudly claimed the Baptist heritage, but interpreted it broadly to include figures such as Walter Rauschenbusch, Harry Emerson Fosdick, and historically important Baptists from England and the continent. Marney sought to be a force for Baptist renewal and to broaden the ecclesiastical and theological bases of the Southern Baptists. He approached that task with determination and humor, knowing that he had to deal with cultural conditioning, parochialism, and fundamentalism. He knew that the Baptist tradition included a "folksiness" that often enabled Baptists to laugh at themselves, and he often played on that humor. He liked to tell the following story to Baptist audiences:

> I once heard of a Quaker farmer in Texas who owned a particularly ill-tempered cow. One morning as he was giving the cow some feed prior to milking, he stood too close to the cow and it bit him. Later as he adjusted his milking stool the cow swatted him with its tail. Finally after he had finished milking, he turned away for a few seconds and the cow kicked over the milk bucket. That was the last straw. The farmer marched around and looked the cow straight in the eye. "Cow," he said, "thou tryest my patience. Thou hast hurt me and angered me. Thou knowest that the principles of my faith keep me from harming thee. What thou dost not know, however, is that I am going to sell thee to a Baptist."

There were also times of family renewal amid Marney's busy schedule. Invitations to speak to cattleworkers on big ranches (probably a distinctively Texas phenomenon) were worked out so that Marney could take his wife and daughters. Horseback riding, long a favorite activity of Marney's, was a shared family event. Marney hunted occasionally with friends, mostly for a change of pace, and on several occasions he even hunted elk and deer in Colorado. Travels to the Yukon and to Latin America refreshed him and gave him new perspectives on other lands and cultures. His daughters, who were preteens during the Austin years, remember family camping trips, visits with family in Tennessee, and their Daddy often being late for dinner. The family enjoyed many cultural events at the University of Texas, and on rare, quiet nights at home, Marney liked to read books about the Civil War. (That great event in American history was Marney's major academic interest — apart from theological matters — during his adult years.)

Several close friends recall that Marney "struggled for faith" during these creative years of ministry, although that is not apparent from reading Marney's sermons of this period. He showed more confidence in laying bare the pretense and pain of the human condition than in providing the traditional answers of faith. It is perhaps more fairly stated that Marney was himself in theological transition during his Austin years. His intellectual liberalism which had once been the answer to conservatism was reshaped by the impact of a developing pastoral theology which was person-centered and oriented to human experience. The "threats" to faith — materialism, scientism, agnosticism — about which he often preached were more than just harmless windmills at which he could tilt and emerge triumphant. They were existential threats, and Marney wrestled with them because they represented formidable obstacles to his own life of faith. A more detailed consideration of this theological struggle will be examined later in Chapter III; suffice it to say here that his theology was integral to his life, and his affirmations arose from his own struggles.

One project close to Marney's heart while he was in Austin was The Marbridge Foundation, established in 1953 to provide Christian rehabilitation for retarded boys and young men. The Foundation purchased a ranch and built various training facilities. Little did Marney realize, when he dedicated an old dairy barn in 1953 to launch the Foundation's work, that his own nephew would become a resident in 1962. Marney remained on the Board of Directors long after he left Austin, and writing to the Directors in 1978 on the 25th anniversary of the founding of Marbridge, he recalled it "the only one of its kind," a place for these children "whose future would always be a special kind of boyhood or girlhood."[12]

After a decade, Marney came to feel that perhaps he had made his contribution to Austin. He knew that in one sense his work there would never be done, and he had a high sense of the future potential of the First Baptist Church. He was comfortable, well-established, and working with a competent staff. His ministerial instincts, however,

---

[12]*The Marbridge Experience,* Vol. 6, No. 3 (September, 1978), p. 2.

told him that when things were going that well it was time to reappraise one's call and the creative edges of ministry. Marney, mindful of his pledge to follow new light whenever it appeared to him, began to assess overtures from other churches as possible sources of new light for a fresh ministry. One such overture — initially declined and then offered again — came from Myers Park Baptist Church in Charlotte, North Carolina. Marney wrestled with the call for some time, then, in 1958, finally accepted. His affection for the First Baptist Church of Austin is reflected in his statement of resignation to the congregation:

> From my sermon, you have gathered what I now must do. I must acknowledge my love for this city and its people who have received me, blessed me and importuned me and mine to stay. We could never have earned this although we have wished never to leave. I must acknowledge the messages I treasure, but have not dared to read. The extraordinary interest and kindness of friends of all faiths, of business and professional people, of men of the press, radio, and television have put me under obligation I cannot pay. Meetings with me and without me of deacons, committees and the congregation, along with the document of dedication produced by these meetings, have put me to great stress of soul. What I now must do occasions the deepest grief I have known thus far, but I believe there is also hidden in this a real joy for us all in due time.
>
> I have been put under a kind of spiritual arrest from within to serve our same cause for the same purpose in another city. Charlotte is a beautiful city too. And Myers Park reflects the power and presence of the great Church to which we all belong. I intend to love Charlotte and Myers Park as I have loved Austin and First Church. God knows I could not love them more. I am not sure why I must do this, for I have not even seen the people, except that I know I will go just as I once knew I would come to Austin. Not once in ten years has this pulpit been less than free. No man has stayed me, and except for my own faltering, ignorance or lack of courage, the Gospel has been preached. Now I go to a pulpit I fully believe to be as free as this one has been. But I do not come down from this one gladly, nor of my own desire, nor by yours, you have said. I do come down because I feel I

must in service to the Gospel of God and the Great Church and I ask for your release of me at the close of this month.[13]

With these words, a decade ended in Marney's life. To keep it in perspective, let us be reminded that it was also the years of McCarthyism, the Korean War, the Eisenhower presidency, the *Brown* decision, television's rapid spread, Chambers and Hiss, rock and roll, Little Rock and the Montgomery bus boycott. The specters of race and right-wing politics haunted the country, creating a troubled climate within which Marney spoke and wrote. His candor and courage, strengthened no doubt by a supportive congregation, heartened many less secure pastors across the South. At a time when the deep South was saying "NEVER" to black stirrings for desegregation, Marney's prophetic preaching in Austin reached many a Christian conscience.

Marney left Austin with a heavy heart. When he was invited to speak at Southwestern Baptist Theological Seminary in Fort Worth a year after he left Austin, he acknowledged his disappointment that there were cleavages in Austin he could not heal and seemed frustrated with his own limitations.[14] These reminiscences, however, seem to be the natural concerns of a minister with great hopes for a congregation. By any professional criteria his ministry there was rich and his impact was felt all over the state. Texas ran in his blood for the rest of his life.

Charlotte: Ecumenical Ministry and National Prominence (1958-1967)

On September 14, 1958, Marney was installed as Senior Minister at Myers Park Baptist Church in Charlotte. The largest city in the Carolinas and practically astride the North Carolina/South Carolina state line, Charlotte proudly heralds herself as the "Queen City of the Carolinas." Prominent in banking, transportation, and textiles, the city has developed a style of church life reflective of middle-class, bourgeois Protestantism. The Presbyterian influence is particularly strong, reinforced by the presence of Queens College in Charlotte and Davidson College just a few miles north.

---

[13]These words are reproduced from Marney's handwritten copy. As far as I can ascertain they were never published.

[14]"We Have This Treasure," an address delivered on July 9, 1959. A tape of the address is available at the Audio-Visual Library of Southwestern Baptist Theological Seminary in Fort Worth.

In 1958, Myers Park Baptist Church was a relatively young congregation, organized to express a more progressive voice within the Southern Baptist Convention. It has a prestigious location in surburban Charlotte and a magnificent physical plant. It was once called "the most formal church in the Southern Baptist Convention".[15] Like several other progressively-oriented Baptist churches, it sought and gained dual affiliation with the American Baptist Convention. Marney's predecessor, Dr. George Heaton, was known for his liberal theology and his emerging interests in labor arbitration. Although the Church did not struggle with Biblical fundamentalism, it had a sizable number of members whose instincts were *economically* conservative. Marney had dealt with people of similar persuasion in Austin, but it was at Myers Park that be began to understand the power of entrenched economic interests. He later observed that Paducah had taught him about poverty, Austin about race, and Myers Park about economics.

The circumstances of Marney's call to Myers Park are intriguing in their own right. The Church, in its own inimitable manner, had established a pulpit committee of fifty people. The committee sought to locate "one of the leading preachers in America," and Marney had been recommended to the committee by various sources, including Robert McCracken, then senior minister of the Riverside Church in New York; James McCord, Dean of Austin Presbyterian Theological Seminary; and Nolan B. Harmon, the Bishop of the Western North Carolina Conference of the Methodist Church. McCord told one member of the pulpit committee that he regarded Marney, ecumenically speaking, as "the greatest preacher in the Southeast," but added that if Marney tried to leave Austin, "I'll break both of his legs."

The booklet about Marney printed by Myers Park makes it clear that Marney was not initially impressed with the Church. He told a preliminary sub-committee that he had heard that Myers Park was a country club church and that he wasn't interested. Only after long and mutually exhausting sessions with the pulpit committee did Marney come to feel that this might be a fruitful place for ministry. When he finally came, as Gene Owens (Marney's successor at Myers Park) put it, "He swaggered in,...trailing mud and horse manure."

Marney had set clear conditions on his call to Myers Park. He

---

[15]Everett Hullum, "One Day in the Life of Southern Baptists," *Home Missions,* February-March, 1978, p. 2.

asked for and received assurances that the Church would (a) recognize the validity of all forms of baptism of persons who presented themselves for church membership, and (b) follow the practice of open communion. He saw this Church and pulpit as a base for an ecumenical ministry; he was no longer interested in supporting parochial patterns of Baptist Church life. Mindful of the growing significance of the race issue, he also got an assurance from the Board of Deacons that no one would be denied membership in the Church on the basis of race. Two of his long-time, trusted associates at Austin— James Berry, his Minister of Music, and William Schwantes, his Church Administrator—were offered positions on the Myers Park Staff.

Methodist Bishop Nolan Harmon preached Marney's Installation sermon on the theme "This Church and the Fellowship of all Christians," and became a good friend of Marney's during the Charlotte years.

Marney's Charlotte debut was not without its tensions. Prominent businessmen soon began to wonder openly just who their pastor was. Marney recalled that after six months, he had not found a single issue on which he and the chairman of the committee which called him could agree. Yet they came to respect each other; the man subsequently defended Marney staunchly against other critics, even to the point of telling them he would pick up the remainder of their pledge for a year if they wanted to leave, but that he was staying.[16]

The resident staff members at Myers Park likewise were apprehensive about working with a "senior" minister whom they hardly knew. They were willing for Marney to be the pulpiteer of the church and to have the high French walnut pulpit—13 steps above the congregation—as his private domain. But they wanted the freedom to pursue their specialized ministries in youth work, children's work, educational programming, and pastoral care consistent with their own training and perspectives. In addition, Marney inherited a situation where some staff people had come to feel that the high pulpit was an empty symbol, and that the true rewards of the Christian life were being explored in other corners of the kingdom. Study groups, social action task forces, growth groups, and prayer groups all formed an important dynamic in the internal life of the church, but at that point

---

[16]"Preaching the Gospel, South of God," p. 918.

in American Protestantism there was considerable question as to the place of the spoken word.

Marney gave his staff freedom to explore their interests, and their admiration grew as they saw his competence in the pulpit. Marney later wrote that he was probably "the sorriest administrator they ever saw," and that his various outside speaking engagements kept him effectively out of the way of creative internal movements. In reflecting on the mission of Myers Park Baptist Church, Marney came to see that the Church needed, as he said, a "barker, a frontman, or even a bellwether" outside the main tent to proclaim to the community that the show inside is worth the price of admission.[17]

Charlotte brought Marney new opportunities and new frustrations. He traveled extensively along the eastern seaboard and renewed ties with old friends from Tennessee and Kentucky. He cautiously eyed, and was eyed in return by, the upper-class world of Charlotte. He found some camaraderie in a ministerial study group under the leadership of Bishop Harmon. (Members of the group included John R. Brokhoff of St. Marks Lutheran Church; Lawrence Stell of Trinity Presbyterian; Willson Weldon of Myers Park Methodist Church; Warner L. Hall of Covenant Presbyterian; Thom W. Blair at Christ Church Episcopal and Carl E. Bates of First Baptist.) They were competent, enlightened men, but Marney found no "soul mates" among Charlotte clergy to compare with his Austin friends Blake Smith and Ed Heinsohn. He also missed his ties with Austin Theological Seminary and the vitality of academically-oriented colleagues. The conventional patterns of church life and the piety of Charlotte were a bit much for this mountain man who liked ideas, vitality, and change. Reflecting back on the Charlotte of 1958, Marney observed that in that Presbyterian haven he found no "community zealots" comparable to his friends in Austin. He further observed: "The Bible Belt and Billy Graham's home town choked on its own salvation. Any 250-year-old Protestant county has few agonies of the spirit that are not involved in some Biblicism or other."[18]

In an address at Southwestern Baptist Theological Seminary shortly after he was settled in Charlotte, Marney described the church

---

[17]These observations were made in an unpublished manuscript of Marney's entitled "Tragic Man - Tragic House," which deals with new visions of the Church and its ministry.

[18]*Ibid.*

Marney the Man | 43

people of Charlotte as:

> ...numerous enough to be a majority;
> established enough to be unchallenged, unthreatened;
> settled enough to need an earthquake to disturb them;
> old enough to begin to want some dignity and poise and
> senile stultification;
> rich enough to be social leaders;
> powerful enough to feel no social pressure;
> pious enough to know no conviction for their sin;
> and complacent enough to feel no real responsibility
> anywhere.[19]

Marney knew that he had work to do in the "Queen City."

Marney slowly grew to appreciate the potential of the Myers Park congregation and they, in turn, came to understand him better. There was, after all, some incongruity in a Tennessee mountain man, seasoned by years in the Southwest, coming to the pulpit of such a socially prominent church, and Marney often joked about it when he was away from Myers Park. He told the story of one of his unrefined Texas rancher friends coming by to see him in Charlotte. Marney gave him a tour of the church, ending up in the sanctuary. The rancher, still wearing his cowboy boots, looked around in awe, gave a low whistle, and finally said, "This place would shore hold a lot of sheep." Marney replied: "It does, Joe, it does."

Marney's ministry at Myers Park eventually turned in a more ecumenical direction, and his competent staff freed him for writing and lecturing. He was restive about denominational labels and increasingly alienated from the power structure of the Southern Baptist Convention. He came to feel that Baptist leaders were usually asking the wrong questions about modern culture, and hence their answers were irrelevant to the deeper problems which plagued the churches. The real threat to the Gospel, Marney came to feel in the Myers Park context, came from the assumptions of upper-middle class life: a complacency which does not hear and is not interested in the cries of the politically powerless and the victims of injustice; a *Sitz im Leben* which never feels the sting of discrimination by race or creed, and presumes that a privileged status naturally reflects God's special favor. These invidious assumptions cross all denominational lines;

---

[19]"We Have This Treasure," *op. cit.*

Marney felt that the Christian community is divided most tragically not by denominational schisms but by the prerogatives of social class and economic privilege. The real task of ministry, he maintained, was not to convince people that they should "believe in Jesus" but to help them see through the ideologies which shape their personal and social consciousness. Marney's volume *Structures of Prejudice* (1961) spoke directly to these issues, but while it was well-received nationally, it drew bitter opposition in Charlotte. Marney was getting too close to the marrow.

Time magazine, in an analysis of Southern Baptists in its October 17, 1960 issue (especially timely because of wide-spread Southern Baptist opposition to the John F. Kennedy candidacy), featured Marney as one of the five leading Baptist preachers in America and pointed out how he dramatically differed from other prominent Baptist leaders. Marney, described as "fiery," was depicted as one who had opposed segregation for years, who practiced open communion at his church, and who dubbed religious opposition to Kennedy as prejudice. *Time* quoted Marney as calling Baptist extremists "Holy Roller Catholics who are creating an emotional authoritarianism which is far more rigid that Roman Catholicism."[20] Marney became increasingly skeptical about the possibilities of changing the denominational image or the posture of the SBC, and yet he continued to exert a formidable influence at Baptist colleges, universities, and seminaries. He stood for the place of alternatives within the Baptist tradition.

The dual union of Myers Park Baptist Church with both the Southern and American Baptist Conventions enabled Marney to take an important step in his own denominational affiliation. After exploring the implications with appropriate officials, Marney applied for and received ministerial standing with the ABC; he also shifted to its retirement plan. He never, as far as I can ascertain, officially repudiated his SBC roots or ties, but it is significant that on the various *vitae* and resumes prepared in the last decade of his life, he listed his denomination as "American Baptist." It is not accidental that his books were published by a Methodist Press (Abingdon) and by an American Baptist Press (Judson).

The Marney years at Myers Park spanned troubling times in America: the election and subsequent assassination of John F.

---

[20]*Ad. loc.*, p. 88.

Kennedy; the exhilaration of a nation committed to space exploration; the Bay of Pigs fiasco; and the increasing tempo of the Civil Rights Movement which particularly rocked the Charlotte-Greensboro area of North Carolina in the early 1960's. Marney addressed those and other national issues with nerve and insight. He thought that the churches of the south had a rare opportunity to provide leadership on the race issue, but later concluded (and stated publicly) that "The Churches of Charlotte don't have enough gas to get from here to Wadesboro." Marney was not himself an activist in these years; he did not go to Selma, for example, or join the "Freedom Rides." He chose to act as interpreter and defender of those on the front lines of social change, feeling it important to be able to communicate with his people. ("If you get too far in front of your people," he once confided to a younger colleague, "they mistake you for the enemy.")

Stories about Marney and the Myers Park Church abound in the "oral tradition." One story gave Marney's explanation of his ongoing tenure in such a wealthy, socially conservative church.

> "Well," drawled Marney in his Tennessee accent, "I've thought about that and have concluded that there are three reasons they don't fire me. The first is that there are some enlightened people on the Board of Deacons. The second is that I've got a strong and supportive staff and we all think about the ministry in the same way."

> "What's the third reason?," his inquirer asked.

> "The church has a million dollar debt. They ain't about to fire me when they have to make those mortgage payments."

Marney's increasing reputation as a pulpiteer brought invitations to speak in the chapels of Duke, Yale, Harvard, Chicago, Vanderbilt, and other leading universities. He lectured widely at seminaries, including repeated appearances in the summer institutes at Princeton Theological Seminary and at Union Seminary in New York City. He also preached several times at the Riverside Church. The armed services continued to call on him to lead seminars for active duty chaplains, and summers inevitably brought invitations to do sermons and lectures at the Chautauqua Institute in New York and at the Massanetta Center in Virginia. (These latter experiences were family events, and Marney found them more renewing than professionally taxing.)

Publications were also forthcoming and well-received across America. His volume *Beggars in Velvet* appeared in 1960; the title had a wry irony for Charlotte. *Structures of Prejudice* was published in 1961 and was a selection of the Religious Book Club, the Psychology Book Club, and the Pulpit Book Club; and *The Recovery of the Person* appeared in 1963. In addition, four volumes of sermons were published during his Myers Park tenure: *He Became Like Us,* 1964; *The Suffering Servant,* 1965; *The Carpenter's Son,* 1967 (a Pulpit Book Club selection); and *The Crucible of Redemption,* 1968. Such productivity was recognized, as one might expect. Marney received a Litt.D. from Wake Forest University in 1963; a D.D. from Johnson C. Smith University in 1964, and another D.D. from Kalamazoo College in 1967.

Such plaudits can be intoxicating, and it is to Marney's credit that he received them modestly. Frequently in private conversations and lectures he acknowledged that Elizabeth was not only his best critic, but also the one who kept him realistic about his faults and honest about his motives. Somehow Marney was able to exist in a world of professional prominence without yielding to its allurements or losing his vision of the prophetic ministry. His ability to laugh at himself and the "passing parade" (as he liked to say) was a healthy corrective to the adulation which came to him.

Although Marney's prominence was related primarily to his speaking and writing for broad audiences, and his staff handled most of the pastoral demands of the congregation, Marney always thought of himself as a pastor as well as a preacher. He increasingly gave the bulk of his counseling time to fellow ministers of all denominations. He knew well the deep hurts and perplexing dilemmas which confront men and women in the ministry, and he recognized that such bruised persons had few places to turn for help. Though never trained in counseling beyond his work in seminary, Marney's friendship with Karl Menninger helped him understand the personal problems of ministers. He knew the defensive facades behind which ministers are inclined to hide. He was often gruff in laying bare those facades, but his rough exterior covered a compassionate spirit. He was known as a "pastor to pastors," and both the nature and complexity of the professional ministry became growing areas of his concern.

Marney was aware of the paradoxes inherent in his privileged place at Myers Park. While he sought to remain a prophetic preacher ("There is no other kind of preaching," he often said), he realized that he was well cared for by his congregation and staff. A prosperous prophet, he once mused, is a contradiction in terms. He tried to be *in* the Myers Park ethos without becoming *of* it; he knew the temptations of comfort, but tried to resist them as a matter of principle. He did not, however, lose his sense of humor. When a ministerial friend from Texas came to Charlotte to preach at Myers Park, Marney gave him a tour of the lovely parsonage, paused to survey the beautiful lawn and grounds, and sighed: "Ah, Lord — I have given up all to follow Thee."

The opportunity for personal renewal during the Charlotte years was closely tied to the purchase of a mountain home outside of Waynesville, North Carólina, a few miles from the United Methodist Assembly Grounds at Lake Junaluska. What had been at one time an old apple storage bin was architecturally re-designed and expanded into an attractive home, to which the Marneys retreated whenever they could. Horses were kept on the property, and riding remained one of Marney's favorite pastimes. This home on Wolf Pen Mountain became the place of convalescence during Marney's illnesses and his permanent home during the last decade of his life.

Marney continued to explore the teachings of Freud for an understanding of the human condition, building on his discovery of Freud during his Austin years. He moved more definitely into a theology of the person, attempting to yoke contemporary theological and psychological insights. He found the more objectified approaches to theology (as seen in Barth and the neo-orthodox movement) too confident and rigid for exploring the deep recesses of the human spirit. More rigorous in his own thought in this period than in Austin, he still continued to walk the borderline between effective preaching and creative theologizing. In the world of American homiletics, Marney was favorably compared to George Buttrick, Ralph Sockman, Paul Scherer, and Edmund Steimle, and his national prominence reached its zenith during his Myers Park days. He was one of two final candidates considered by the President and Fellows of Harvard to succeed George Buttrick as Preacher to the University and Pastor of the Memorial Church. "As a preacher," observed one person familiar with the national scene, "Marney had few peers and no superiors."

There is little doubt, however, that in some areas of the country Marney still had to struggle against his identification as a Southern Baptist. One source indicated that this ecclesiastical and cultural background weighed against Marney in the final deliberations concerning the Harvard post. Stereotypes die slowly, even (Marney might say especially) in sophisticated circles. At this point in his career Marney was no longer typically "southern" or "Baptist." He insisted, in fact, that "Baptist" is an adjective, not a noun. Although the Southern Baptist tradition gave Marney his roots, his studies, curiosity, humanity, and experience all impelled him into broader arenas, so that ultimately only an ecumenical theology would suffice.

The pace of Marney's life stunned his associates and concerned his family. In addition to making frequent appearances on college and university campuses, he was also in great demand to speak at church gatherings, state councils of churches, ministers' retreats, and special programs of local churches. Driven by something which he apparently did not fully understand himself, Marney continued to accept so many invitations that Charlotte was often simply a resting point between engagements. A full-time administrator at Myers Park Baptist Church relieved Marney of most of the tedious details of church administration, and his staff provided a creative internal ministry. But his body couldn't sustain the pace. Marney suffered a heart-attack in September 1966. The attack incapacitated him for a long period of time, and his recovery was further complicated by lung surgery and a colon difficulty. After serious conversations with his wife and a few close friends, Marney finally decided that he could no longer serve as senior minister of the Myers Park Baptist Church. On Good Friday 1967, he wrote the following to his Board of Deacons:

Beloved Community:

It is time today to give answer to the gracious letter the Deacons sent last September. I have carried it seven months, with its assurances and its gracious insistence that all the time I should need was mine. I am profoundly grateful for it, as for the hundreds of more private expressions that have come. Now I see my way, and to take more of your generosity would be hurtful for you and prolong the strain of uncertainty on me.

First, I must say this: My situation is in no way an effect of the pastorate of Myers Park Baptist Church. No people ever made less demand; none were ever easier to serve; no staff was ever better formed, and work was never better divided. Nor is there anywhere a more precious and effective local community. I found Church with you and all my ways and days will bear the mark of what you gave me, taught me, suffered me to learn among you.

Circumstances utterly beyond my control or desire turn me from you. I have literally preached myself into the contradiction which now requires my resignation, or I become denier of the light and a castaway. You have heard me vow to follow any new light I could get; you have known me to be a candidate for any post that would put me nearer the center of the sea of troubles that now beset the Great Church; and you heard me find my way to the Interpreter's House. This is where I must abide for now. I shall be trying to live among the clergy and laity of a vast region in an Interpreter's House at Lambuth Inn, Lake Junaluska, just what I have learned from the Interpreter's House I found at Myers Park Baptist Church. Such a joy as we have had *must* be one that will share well.

Did ever a man preach himself out a of a dearer, lovelier place? I would have stayed with you, and fattened on your generosity forever, except for last September. And now you must do two things: you must be Church, and you must gladly let me go. I have done all I know to you. My resignation should take effect at once, though I confess that every day, Sundays especially, and every Holy Week in particular, I shall long for Camelot and wish I were back . So will Elizabeth to whom you are dear.

I did not come willingly to your high pulpit—and as all of you know, I did not come down willingly or wistfully. You might say I was carried in, and carried out. But the years in between? They are treasured lodes of conflict, learning, growth, and loss, too. "Such a sleep they sleep, those men I loved."

You are Church, with or without anybody. And where I go it is in your name and The Name I have learned to say better while among you. I shall be close enough to hear of and rejoice in the children. My constant love is to them—as to you.

I rejoice now in this strange new turn for which all my life has prepared me. But if any ever preaches any other gospel to you, "Let him be anathema!"

In love,

Carlyle Marney

The *Charlotte Observer,* editorializing about the years of Marney's ministry in Charlotte, reminded its readers that Marney once observed that "Southern churches of all denominations are mainly Jesus cults dressed in the Little Lord Fauntleroy clothing of our confederate narcissism." It also recalled Marney's sadness that the first steps toward integration in Charlotte were taken by the Chamber of Commerce and not by the churches. Perhaps the *Observer's* most pointed observation was its acknowledgement that "Marney gave us no peace—but then again, we didn't deserve any."

A Minister to Ministers: The Interpreter's House (1967-1978)

During Marney's last years at Myers Park he was drawn to the model of the church as an "Interpreter's House," a term drawn from John Bunyan's *Pilgrim's Progress*. In Bunyan's vision, the church would be a place for rest, renewal, instruction, and self-integration; in short, "a house for the relief of Pilgrims." Marney sensed especially the need for such a place for those bruised or broken by the ministry. During the days of his convalescence from his heart attack, Marney began to formalize his thoughts about this project and approached several foundations, the United Methodist Church, and the American Baptist Convention about its viability. It was for Marney a dream, a new frontier in ministry, and an alternative to the incessant pressures of his Myers Park life.

With the help of foundation grants and denominational support, the Interpreter's House at Lake Junaluska, North Carolina, became a reality in 1967, with Marney its founder-director. Lake Junaluska was well-known in the Southeast as a Methodist Conference Center in the lap of the Smokey Mountains; it was proximate to Marney's own mountain home at Wolf Pen Mountain and allowed Marney to achieve personal, geographical, and professional integration. Working space for the Interpreter's House was provided by Lambuth Inn, one of the old hotels at the Lake Junaluska assembly grounds. Marney invited Erna Alsdurf, his long-time secretary from Myers Park Baptist Church, to join him, and also asked a young Harvard Ph.D., James W. Fowler, to venture with him in the Interpreter's House enterprise.

This move in Marney's professional career marked a great transition on many fronts. It was, first of all, a pilot project in ministry to ministers. For the first time in years, he was no longer a parish minister, but rather operated on broad inter-denominational fronts. He seemed to welcome the relief from the constant preaching demands of addressing a local congregation, but the pace of his life scarcely slackened because he continued to accept so many outside speaking engagements. Even when he knew it would be wise to limit his engagements, he felt a need to describe his hopes for the Interpreter's House to a wide variety of ministerial audiences. The plan for the development of the Interpreter's House was simple: to publicize its existence in denominational and interdenominational journals; to invite those with hurts, or in personal or professional transitions, to come; to obtain financial aid for persons without adequate funds of their own; to plan personal and group therapy sessions, and to provide appropriate trained leadership. Sessions varied in length, and leadership rotated. Manual labor on the grounds of the Lake Junaluska Assembly provided a break from the intense mental and emotional sessions. The program began modestly, but quickly expanded as it became better known. Eventually lay persons as well as ministers were included in its scope.

Marney carried much of the leadership load himself during the first few years, but later assumed responsibilities for fund-raising, long-range planning, leadership recruitment, and publicity. But almost always, he spent some time with each group who came, and when he had the time he became vigorously involved in the program. The Interpreter's House received national attention through the special program devoted to it by Bill Moyers on Public Television on December 26,1973.

As we shall see in more detail in Chapter IV, Marney's theology and ecclesiology changed during his eleven years with the Interpreter's House. He grew more openly critical of denominational structures and was drawn deeply into intensive group therapy and personal counseling with both clergy and lay people. Through this ministry, his person-centered theology developed during his Myers Park years was now put into practice. Marney also extended his theological boundaries to take more seriously the interaction of Christians with Jews, Muslims, and all persons of good will. His persistent theme in this period of time was the notion of a *Higher Good:* "a vision which can transcend the parochial limitations and selfish instincts which all persons and groups have."

Marney worked on social and political fronts during his last decade, but not as a front-line activist. In years which were turbulent with student unrest, anti-Vietnam protests, the bombing of Cambodia, economic depression, and Watergate, he perceived these political upheavals as symptoms of a deeper malaise: the lack of clear priorities, both individually and nationally; the egocentrism of institutions; the hypocrisy of power; and the festering needs of marginal people in society. Political engagement *per se* is not the answer, he asserted time and again; we must have a new vision of humanity. Too often, Marney cautioned, we become so preoccupied with immediate *problems* that we cannot discern the deeper *issues* which are at stake in the modern world.

Marney once estimated that through workshops, counseling sessions, and therapy programs over eleven years, the Interpreter's House reached 4500 pastors of 34 denominations, representing 47 states and 4 countries. In addition, some 3500 women, 5000 blacks, and 3400 lay persons took part in the programs of the Interpreter's House. It is regrettable that soon after Marney's death the Interpreter's House was closed. Faced with increasing operating costs, its Board of Directors decided that without Marney's fund-raising efforts the project could not be sustained. In some ways that decision acknowledged that Marney's own personal magnetism was the critical ingredient of the Interpreter's House. In other ways, it reflected the fact that the work of the Interpreter's House was paralleled increasingly by university and seminary programs of continuing education for ministers.

Marney produced a number of provocative papers which explored a new vision of the church and the type of minister necessary in a rapidly changing age, but he was not as productive in his writing output as he was during his Myers Park tenure. That may have reflected a lack of support staff; it also undoubtedly resulted from a more intensive engagement in personal counseling and a heavy load of speaking and preaching engagements. It is sobering to note, in fact, that the heavy professional load which clearly was a part of Marney's health problems at Myers Park soon crept back on him, and one who studies his professional calendar notes little difference between the years of 1974-78 and 1963-67. Against the advice of family and close friends, Marney never eased up on his professional schedule. A lifelong friend observed that it was as though Marney was "driven." Knowing that death was an ever-present reality, Marney was determined, as he remarked to one friend, to "die with his boots on." Professionally he felt the weight of keeping the Interpreter's House going; psychologically it was easier for him to preach about *being* rather than *doing* than it was to implement that in his own life and schedule. The two books written by Marney during his Interpreter's House years were *The Coming Faith* (Abingdon, 1970) and *Priests to Each Other* (Judson Press, 1974).

The Interpreter's House years were also years of new teaching responsibilities. From 1972 to 1978 Marney served as Adjunct Professor of Preaching at the Duke Divinity School, commuting from his home in the mountains to the Duke campus during one semester each academic year. In 1976 he also spent one term as a Visiting Professor of Humanities at the Virginia Military Institute, an institution not noted for its emphasis on humanistic studies. Marney lectured on broad interdisciplinary themes relating the condition of modern man to the changing dynamics of modern life and was well received in his teaching. Elizabeth Marney reports that he found the experience at V.M.I. "exhilarating," and likened his classroom encounters there to his teaching days at Austin Theological Seminary.

In the last two years of his life, Marney received two professional tributes to his continued creativity and influence. He was awarded a D.D. from the University of Glasgow in 1976, partially in recognition of his homiletical and theological contributions over the years, but primarily to honor his work at The Interpreter's House. The degree citation called the Interpreter's House "one of the most significant rehabilitative centers in the North American continent." Marney, I was told, was the first American pastor (as opposed to an academic theologian) since Harry Emerson Fosdick to be honored with a Glasgow D.D. The other honor was Yale's invitation to him to deliver the prestigious Beecher Lectures on Preaching in 1980. Marney was at work on those lectures when he died; he intended to relate his experiences at the Interpreter's House to the preaching task of the minister.

Marney's friends and associates noted personality changes in his last few years. He was less patient with and charitable towards those of conservative theological persuasion; he was openly irritated by fundamentalists, whom he likened to "people driving Amish buggies down Interstate highways." He could be acerb in group interaction. He suffered from occasional depressions and was not always pleased when he reflected on the results of his thirty-year ministry. Some of these changes may have been related to the impact of his health problems and the aging process; some may have been rooted in an awareness that his own time was running out, and he had not accomplished all he had hoped.

Marney's strenuous schedule continued until July 3, 1978, the day of his death. He was stricken with a heart attack while working in his office at Lake Junaluska, preparing a set of lectures for a Pastor's

Convocation of 600 ministers to be held at Furman University. Just a few months before his death he delivered a major address at Union Seminary in New York, commemorating the one-hundredth anniversary of Fosdick's birth. In those last months several friends sensed that Marney knew he had abused his body and was living on borrowed time. In his last published sermon, preached in the Duke Chapel, Marney seemed to be prescient of his death. He concluded that sermon with the following words, which were later read at his funeral by Robert E. McClernon, his long-time colleague at Myers Park:

> If, entering now the zenith of my brief arc around and within creation, I should enter God's great Assize hall tomorrow, called to account for myself, I should offer this Confession and Defense, if indeed I could do more than fall down. But if able to give vocal response at all, I should say this:

> Thou knowest, dear Lord of our Lives, that for fifty of thy-my years, in ignorance, zest, zeal, and sin, I lived as if Creation and I had no limit. I lived, and wanted, and was, as if I had forever —without regard for time, or wit, or strength, or need, or limit or endurance, and as if sleep were a needless luxury and digestion an automatic process. But Thou, O Lord of real love, didst snatch my bits and ride me into Thy back-pasture and didst rub my nose in my vulnerability and didst split my lungs into acquiescence, and didst freeze my colon in grief loss, and didst press me into that long depression at the anger I directed against myself and didst press me to knee-drop where the only word of petition I could utter was a despair-ridden "open, open," and Thou didst read over my shoulder my diary of that long journey when I did melt before Thee as mere Creature. Thou, then, didst hear.

> Hear, now, my pitiable defense: In all my sixty years I killed no creature of thine I did not need for food except for a few rattlesnakes, a turtle or two, two quail I left overlong in my coat, and three geese poisoned, before I shot them, on bad grain in Nebraska, plus one wood-duck in Korea. In all my years, I consciously battered no child — though my own claim much need to forgive me — and consciously misused no person. Thou knowest my aim to treat no human as thing — never to hate overlong — to pass no child without his-her

eye, and my innermost wish to love as Thou dost love by seeing no shade of color or class. And Thou didst long ago hear my cry to let me go from Paducah. Thou knowest my Covenant with Elizabeth in our youth and Thou knowest it has been better kept than my Covenant with Thee, and willst thou forgive? Indeed, thou hast. Hear now my intention with Grace as if it were fact. I do and have intended to be Responsible in Creation by Covenant, and where I have defaulted do Thou forgive. Forgive thou my vicarious responsibilty for all the defection from thy purpose of all thy responsible creatures, and accept Thou this my admission of utter dependence upon Thy mercy.

. . . "Naked came I into the world." How I'm dressed at conclusion makes no difference: a pair of jeans or a Glasgow robe - it makes no difference. Meantime? I mow, I cut wood for winter, I clean drainage ditches, I preach what is happening and I listen, and wait, and want, and work, and look to see what God will do in the Earth, His limited Creation which asks for Covenant-response and glories in Redemption as a way-station enroute to Completion. Selah! I watch out always for babies, and little rabbits in front of my mower, and old folks near by, and black snakes worth preserving, and little puppies on the road and the young-old who stutter and lack, and can hear, too, the cry of us all,

Come, Lord Jesus!

Marney's funeral was held on July 5, 1978 at the Myers Park Baptist Church in Charlotte. He was buried, at his wife's request, in his crimson Glasgow robe. Memorial services were also held at Duke and at Princeton. His alienation from the Southern Baptist Convention is symbolized by the fact that his death was only noted in passing by short paragraphs in the state Baptist newspapers of Texas and North Carolina.

A review of Marney's life based solely on an account of his professional career would be inexcusably one-dimensional. Strengthening and enriching the tapestry of his life was his relationship with his wife Elizabeth — a life mate of 38 years. She shared the vicissitudes of his life, cared for him in sickness and in health, and, Marney often said, knew him better than any living being. She was a midwife to many of his deeper self-understandings, and the model to whom he was referring when he said that we could take serious journeys inward only when we are guided by one who loves us. The *LondonTimes* reports in its famous obituary section on the achievements of prominent people and then, almost as an afterthought, puts in a last sentence noting whether or not the person was married. That style would not do justice to Marney's life or personality. Those who knew him knew the importance of Elizabeth to him at all ages and stages of his life. Daughters too—as small children, teen-agers, and grown women—were essential parts of his caring, humor, and being. He was who he was in and through his family.

Five days short of his sixty-second birthday, the pilgrimage of this Southern sojourner ended. A premature death, most people felt, because Marney still had much to do; yet by most standards it was a life filled with zest, adventure, achievement, personal growth, and new visions. He was, someone once said, "a mountaineer with the soul of a poet." Southern born and Southern educated, he lived out his entire life in the South. When I asked Erna Alsdurf what Marney wrote about the South, she paused for a moment and then replied, "Marney didn't really write much about the South—he was the South."

Against this background—Marney's pilgrimage and the context in which he lived and died—let us now consider the evolution of Marney's thought, turning initially to his contributions while a pastor in Austin and Charlotte. How did this pilgrim progress in the realm of ideas?

CHAPTER III

MARNEY AS PASTOR-THEOLOGIAN

All my life I have been seeking another way to be a true believer.

—Marney

Holiness is a strong perfume and a little of it goes a long way in the world. I have never been very clear whether it was compatible with laughter, and I should be very loathe to bid an eternal farewell to laughter.

—W. MacNeile Dixon, *The Human Situation*, p. 14.

As we noted in Chapter II, Marney achieved national prominence in the years 1948-67, spanning the time of his pastorates in Austin and Charlotte. During this time he was essentially a pastor-theologian, and in this chapter we shall limit our assessment to that period of his life. Although the books he published in this period extended his thought and influence to wider audiences, it is fair to say that Marney first drew attention because of his speaking ability. His deep, husky voice, coupled with his sense of humor, timing, and ability to illustrate complex ideas with stories and metaphors, entranced audiences. Like other skilled preachers to whom he has been compared—Steimle, Sockman, Buttrick—he had learned well the art of communication. He knew how to get the attention of an audience, how to touch their emotions, how to lead them along in the process of argument. As a pastor-theologian (distinct from an academic-theologian), Marney kept persons in mind, and tried in both his sermons and his writing to remain concrete, specific and life-oriented. Most of his books emerged from his work in sermons, discussion groups, and talks at retreats and ministers' conferences. His writing was clear and pungent, but most people who knew Marney or ever heard him speak agreed that he had to be heard to be appreciated. "He had a voice like God's," said one acquaintance, "only deeper."

Marney's professional role as a pastor and preacher must be kept in mind as we consider his theological orientation. As we noted in Chapter II, Marney was himself evolving during his years in Austin and Charlotte. His own age span went from 32 to 52: his life circumstances changed from economic marginality to upper-middle class status; daughters grew up and left the nest; his habitat in the southwest gave way to a home in the Carolinas. A growing comprehension of the systemic nature of poverty, the deep and crippling tentacles of racism, and the parochialism of economic self-interests gave an urgency to his reflection. As we consider his basic theological stance over this period of time, we should not be surprised to find an evolutionary pattern and a growing impatience with traditional Christian questions and answers.

For all of Marney's transitions in this twenty-year period, we would do well at the outset to acknowledge some constant factors. He remained persuaded that the Christian revelation had a distinctive message for all persons struggling for meaning and purpose, but he resisted all attempts to simplify or trivialize the kerygma. He opposed all pretense and hypocrisy perpetrated in the name of religion. He repudiated the division of persons into the elect and the damned or the righteous and the sinner. He persistently tried to get his hearers and readers to look beyond themselves and to identify with the plight of those less fortunate. He always felt uneasy about denominational loyalties which undercut a fundamental loyalty to the cause of Christendom. He read widely in and drew heavily upon a broad range of humanists, philosophers, and secular historians.

The variety of Marney's writings is also worth noting. He wrote about mothers and sons, terrible teenagers, faith and doubt, Machiavelli and politics, the Church and liturgy, Christology, homosexuality, Southern culture, Freud, prejudice, education, nationalism, music, and a host of other themes. Marney's grasp of the sheer diversity of life, his familiarity with the quandaries of human experience, his dual role as nurturer of a congregation and Christian apologist to despisers of the faith, his painful recognition of the reality of evil in both political and ecclesiastical processes: all these kept Marney from the cloistered life or from ivory—tower intellectualism. The sweep of his work complicates the task of systematically appraising Marney as a theologian. Nonetheless, there is a basic theological orientation which informs all his writing and preaching from 1948-67, and this chapter will concentrate on those major themes.

Intellectual Influences

In his first major book *Faith in Conflict* (1957), Marney recongnized a number of thinkers "whose music I have used as if it were my own," adding that he took from them "at the price of a diligent ear."[1] He listed Wolfgang Goethe, Friedrich Nietzsche, Nikolai Berdyaev, Soren Kierkegaard, W. Macneile Dixon, John Donne, Fedor Dostoevsky, Paul Tillich, William Temple, G. B. Shaw, Radoslav Tsanoff, Reinhold Niebuhr, Emil Brunner, Martin Luther, and Alfred North Whitehead. He also acknowledged his indebtedness to on-going debates with W. J. Kilgore, Fred Ginascol, Blake Smith, and his brother Milton (whose scientific interests we noted in Chapter I). He acknowledged in later writing still other sources of inspiration. He frequently cited Charles Darwin, Thomas Carlyle, John MacMurray, Thomas Mann, William McNeile Poteat, and H. R. Niebuhr. Like most creative thinkers, however, Marney drew from many sources and was beholden to none. He cannot be categorized as being predominantly under any single influence. He never played the role of disciple, but rather took what he liked or found applicable from different thinkers. He seldom engaged in a sustained critical analysis of another thinker. Undoubtedly Marney's preaching interests and pastoral orientation diminished the time he had available for critical theological analysis; he was not interested in pursuing theology as a formal discipline within western intellectual history. The only exceptions I found to this general theological stance were his penetrating lecture on Walter Rauschenbusch, delivered at the University of Chicago in 1957 to commemorate the centennial of Rauschenbusch's birth, and a similar lecture he gave at Union Theological Seminary in 1978 on Harry Emerson Fosdick.

---

[1] *Op. cit.*, pp. 153-4.

It is clear, however, that several thinkers shaped his perceptions more than others. Luther especially looms large in Marney's theological orientation. (A complete set of Luther's works was located on his study shelves within reach of his desk.) Marney agreed with Luther that humanity is *simul justus et peccator,* and that there is no escape, even for the man or woman of faith, from the demons of pride, ego, selfishness and hypocrisy. As a consequence, he was ruthless in his analysis of the human condition, exposing the human penchant for self-aggrandizement. Marney also felt with Luther that we dare to address God and to deal with life not because we are worthy but because God is gracious. (That insight was important to Marney's own lifestyle as well as to his stance as a theologian and ethicist.) Marney drew heavily upon Luther's concept of vocation*(Beruf)* and (especially in his later years) upon Luther's sense of the priesthood of all believers. In the galaxy of sixteenth century thinkers—Luther, Calvin, Zwingli, Knox, Cranmer, Melanchthon—who molded the Protestant tradition, Luther is the only one to whom Marney refers with any regularity, and the only one to whom he is clearly indebted. Marney said as much about himself as about the Christian tradition when he observed in his later years that Christianity has only had three great interpreters: Paul, Augustine, and Luther.

Marney owed special debts to a cluster of twentieth century British thinkers—in particular W. Macneile Dixon and John MacMurray, but also P.T. Forsyth, John Oman, Herbert Farmer, and William Temple. Dixon's 1937 Gifford lectures, published as *The Human Situation,*[2] had an enormous impact on Marney because of Dixon's attempt to deal honestly with all facets of human experience and his pinpointing of the ambiguities of many religious assertions. Dixon was not technically a theologian—he was Professor of English Language and Literature at the University of Glasgow—but his clever, cogent, and articulate perceptions, revealing an honest but skeptical humanism, struck Marney as more profound and helpful than most Christian writings on human nature. Marney once called Dixon "the prose poet laureate of realism," and in another context called Dixon's *Human Situation* his "private Bible."[3]

---

[2]London: Edward Arnold and Co., 1937.

[3]See *Structures of Prejudice,* p. 59, and a later sermon, "The True Believer" (N.D., mimeographed), p. 2.

Marney, for me, is the door through which "A" will gain access to all these other thinkers.

John MacMurray's Gifford Lectures at Glasgow in 1953 and 1954, published in the two volumes *The Self as Agent* and *Persons in Relation*,[4] confirmed and deepened Marney's instincts that theology ultimately had to deal with the "field of the personal": the self, persons in relationship to each other, and the nature of the human personality. MacMurray tried to analyze the implications of this position for systematic theological reflection, and, as we shall see, Marney follows him at every major point. Most importantly, MacMurray called for a unity of thought and action, showed the sterility of dogmatic or academic theology, and defended the concept of God as a personal, infinite Agent who is engaged with the world. He held that all theological systems required a constant revision and continual verification in action.[5] It is true that Marney was thinking along similar lines before MacMurray's two volumes came into print, but Marney had read MacMurray's earlier works[6] and obviously felt supported by the fundamentals of MacMurray's thought.

In P.T. Forsyth, whom Emil Brunner once called "the greatest of the British theologians." Marney saw the power of paradox and dialectical thinking, and the ability to point powerfully to God without getting ensnared with biblical literalism or dogmatic formalism. Forsyth's compelling depiction of the wonder and majesty of God influenced Marney far more than did the oft-heralded work of Karl Barth. Marney also appreciated Forsyth's stress on humanistic thought and the place of reason, in contrast to Barth's heavy emphasis on revelation. Forsyth's poetic gifts and use of the witty epigram were especially appealing to Marney's temperament.

John Oman's *Grace and Personality*[7] and William Temple's *Nature, God and Man*[8] made their impact on Marney: Oman for the rich way in which he recovered the theme of grace and tied it to a personal God, and Temple for the social vision which led him to affirm a "commonwealth of value" binding all persons, communities, and nations. In his unique role as church leader and theologian, Temple epitomized for Marney the role of the responsible theologian in the

---

[4]London: Faber and Faber, 1957 and 1961.

[5]*Persons in Relation*, p. 223.

[6]Particularly *Reason and Emotion* (1935) and *The Structure of Religious Experience* (1936).

[7]Cambridge: University Press, 1919.

[8]London: Macmillan and Co., 1934.

service of the church. More could be said about the importance of these thinkers in Marney's development, but suffice it to say here that in a rare way among American theologians of his period, Marney showed a familiarity with, and owed debts to, this group of British thinkers. I have found no special clue to this British connection inasmuch as Marney did not study or travel in England, but he seemed to take a special interest in following the published Gifford lectures, and found rich resources in the British tradition.

On the American theological scene, Marney drew from both Reinhold and H. Richard Niebuhr, as indeed did practically every constructive American theologian of his generation. Marney's own *Sitz im Leben* differed from both of them, of course, but as early as his Paducah days he took from Reinhold Niebuhr's *Moral Man and Immoral Society* insights into the inadequacy of an individualist ethic when addressing problems of systemic injustice. In both his sermons and writings he drew from Niebuhr's *Nature and Destiny of Man,* finding in that classic work, with its emphasis on human sinfulness, an analysis which laid bare the human condition without pretense or piety. From H. Richard Niebuhr, Marney drew more from the oft-neglected but important *The Meaning of Revelation* than from Niebuhr's better known writings on culture and the sociology of religion. As Marney looked back on his own theological pilgrimage from a later time in his life, he wrote:

> Here, at this sharp edge of concern (how to understand what "revelation" means in a time when truths have to be reformed) the teacher for me has been Richard Niebuhr. I suspect that if I have become, in my adult years, a true believer, the mid-wife for my birthing has been his *Meaning of Revelation*... Without his *Meaning of Revelation* I simply could not do. He has furnished my understanding of revelation as a being converted... during a revelation.[9]

Tutors from the Baptist tradition are not always as visible but were nevertheless present in Marney's theological orientation. As we noted in Chapter II, Marney had ambivalent feelings about his Baptist heritage and was embarrassed about the Southern Baptist penchant for fundamentalism and parochialism. He knew, however, that there had been a cluster of Baptist thinkers who had made a substantial

---

[9]Mimeographed lecture on "The Language of Revelation," N.D., p. 2.

Some issues: yet audience is smaller & in need of more "remedial" work. Less need for combative language. (More Craddock-like.)

Marney as Pastor-Theologian / 63

contribution to Christian life and thought, and within the American context, Marney felt that the pivotal figure was Walter Rauschenbusch. He discovered Rauschenbusch while a student at Southern Baptist Seminary and turned to him repeatedly in the course of his own ministry when he struggled with problems of Christianity and the social order. Marney once observed about Rauschenbusch:

> Throughout my first twenty-three years I knew only one Southerner who understood Rauschenbusch, and he was a Chicago Ph.D. and therefore suspect. But today if you can scratch a liberal American Protestant and find Rauschenbusch under the surface, don't forget to scratch a Southerner, too, for Walter Rauschenbusch is there wherever the conscience hurts.[10]

Among Rauschenbusch's enduring contributions, Marney cited his analysis of the virility of the Kingdom of Evil, his demand for a responsible society of Christians (emphasizing that the Church could not abdicate the struggle for justice to political institutions and parties), and his stress on the corporate nature of salvation.[11] Marney knew that there were limitations in Rauschenbushs's theology, but there is no doubt that all his professional life he looked to Rauschenbusch as a model of courage and conviction. He once said that along with John Bunyan, Rauschenbusch might be one of the two Baptists remembered over 500 years.[11]

Also in the Baptist tradition, Marney was a great admirer of Harry Emerson Fosdick, defending to his southern audiences Fosdick's insights and integrity, borrowing on occasion (who didn't?) Fosdick's sermon illustrations, and sensing that Fosdick—himself also a pastor-theologian—may well have been the most winsome and influential American interpreter of Christianity in the twentieth century. Marney appreciated Fosdick's wide-ranging intellectual interests, his openness to diverse streams of culture, his honesty, his Biblical foundations, and his theological stress on Personality. Among Fosdick's many books, Marney especially esteemed *The Meaning of Faith*, *The Lordship of Christ*, and *The Forgiveness of Sin*. I have previously suggested that Marney can be compared to Fosdick in his similarity of professional

---

[10]Unpublished lecture on "The Significance of Walter Rauschenbusch," delivered at the University of Chicago, November 4, 1957; p. 2.

[11]*Ibid.*, p. 11.

concerns, his preaching gifts, and his Baptist background; it was fitting that Union Theological Seminary in New York invited Marney to give the major address in the spring of 1978 as that institution celebrated the centennial of Fosdick's birth.[12]

Not all of Marney's intellectual debts, of course, were owed to theologians. He was impressed with the scientific revolution, and in particular with the creative work of Charles Darwin and A.N. Whitehead. Darwin was an especially important figure to Marney, emotionally as well as intellectually, for Darwin's work loomed large behind the Scopes trial and he became a symbol in the modernist-fundamentalist controversy. Marney probed Darwin's work carefully as he wrote his memoir of the Scopes Trial and as he prepared his chapter on "Science" in *Structures of Prejudice*. He was convinced that it was not Darwin but a host of later interpreters, such as Herbert Spencer, who misapplied the theory of evolution. Marney was moved by Darwin's integrity, meticulous methodology, and modest claims for his own work. Darwin also impressed upon him at an early age the importance of scientific inquiry and the value of scientific information; it is only when limited scientific methodologies become dogmatic that "Scientism" emerges as a crippling ideology. Marney retained a healthy respect for science all of his professional career; it caused him to be cautious in speaking theologically of the creation, and, on the whole, to eschew the long warfare between Christianity and Science.

Whitehead's work was likewise important for Marney, primarily because of his interpretation of the world as being in process, and because of the creative way that he worked out a consistent metaphysical theory with a sophisticated sense of science. Marney frequently quoted from Whitehead's *Science and the Modern World*, and in his own words affirmed change and not stasis as the critical metaphysical principle. Marney, let us be clear, was never a "Process Theologian" in the contemporary sense of the term, but he regarded several of Whitehead's concepts as valuable for the modern pastor-theologican. One of these, as we shall see later, dealt with the nature of God.

One could profitably explore Marney's debts to several of the great humanists of the western intellectual tradition—Goethe and

---

[12]Marney's lecture on that occasion, entitled "Apology to Fosdick," is unpublished as of this writing. It apparently will not be published in *The Union Seminary Quarterly Review*. I located a copy of the address in Marney's files.

Shaw come to mind—but we concentrate on one: Sigmund Freud. The discovery of Freud revolutionized Marney's sense of what it means to be a human being. The reality of the unconscious, and the ever-present influence of the *Id* (by whatever name or symbol it is described), mean that human actions and motives can never be understood without the depthful probing of human *inwardness*. Marney was intrigued with Freud's 1917 dictum:

> The Ego (I) is not master in its own house. The conscious mind is mastered from behind it.

Reflecting back on his intellectual debts at a later stage in his career, Marney observed:

> Most of what I have learned, been and done since 1946 when I finished with the history of Christian thought as a discipline, rises from taking Freud's dictum seriously.[13]

Marney, as we shall see, had many different theological concerns over the span of his ministry, but he was always intensely interested in persons. On that central issue, two thinkers molded his thought more than any others: Luther and Freud. *What Luther was to him theologically, Freud was to him psychologically.*

Our intent in this preliminary analysis has been to clarify some of Marney's theological roots and depths. Marney did not appear on America's theological scene indifferent to the broader intellectual currents of his generation. No single thinker or school of thought "explains" Marney; his genius lay in his ability to creatively synthesize from a variety of sources and to intepret complex issues in ways that non-theologians could understand. Having looked into the wells from which he drank, let us now turn to a consideration of his own theological contributions.

The Human Situation

The human dilemma, in Marney's view, is one of contradiction. Outward appearances falsify inward realities. Great gaps exist between what we say and what we are. We live behind masks, pursue illusions and (as Macneile Dixon said) "blow bubbles" to inflate our self-esteem. Marney stressed this theme persistently through two decades. In a sermon in Austin on December 5, 1954, he came at it as follows:

---

[13]"Our Present Higher Good," a sermon preached at Duke and Harvard in 1973 (mimeographed). p. 2.

Contradiction is a thing that is native to us all. For the curse of mankind is the curse of the contradiction in our souls; it makes us act as we would not act and makes it possible for there to be such a broad base of potential within the moral lives of each of us. This is what I mean: I'm saying that it is within the moral potential of every living being, every living nation, every living culture, it's in the actuality of us all that a man may look like a gentleman and be a devil, and that a woman may dress like a queen and have a harlot heart; that a man may have all the education that his calling requires and at the same time be literally obliterated of any thought of permanent significance in his own lifetime by the prejudices that squeeze and constrict him. A man may be gracious and suave and a gentleman on the one hand, and yet somewhere there will appear that glaring inconsistency that just doesn't measure up to what he looks like he is. Contradiction is everywhere. The healthy section of human tissue will frequently house the malignancies that bring seeds of decay in it, and vice versa. The thing that looks as if it has no eternal merit may have some eternal purpose wrapped up in it. We live in this mighty contradiction everywhere, it splits us open. That man who measures the infinite horizon with his mind loses a gland the size of a peanut and becomes an idiot. That man who dreams of eternity and asks eternal questions that he cannot answer gets cold and dies when a germ he cannot even see bites him. The contradiction is all through life. It's everywhere: where men are men and women are women — we live with these split hearts of ours.

Six years later, in a published work geared to a larger audience, he continued to explore the incongruities of life.

Man the full, grand one is also and simultaneously a little man. The one who can create can kill. The historian who remembers is frequently the play actor who pretends; the honorable one is sometimes especially tiresome. The ingenious and skillful craftsman is in the same body also the plunderer; and that one who longs and desires is also the idle, lazy one; while man the wise is simultaneously man the foolish one — and eventually, everywhere, *homo-erector*, the upright one, becomes *homo-crepitans*, the creaking, rattling one, if he lives. Meantime he can so easily become man the *dead one*. If a germ bites, if a gland like a peanut withers, if a valve closes; or if he is punctured or jolted; if he misjudges time, space or speed; if he eats too much or too little, or waits long enough between breaths, he *dies*, we call it, and begins to turn to mineral. Yet he lives like a god, and his deepest grief, desire, agony is that he cannot be God. He lives in a mighty contradiction! And the chaos we decry lives within us.[14]

Contradiction, confusion, hypocrisy, anxiety: these are the deepest characteristics of our humanity. Marney hammered at them relentlessly. Freud's influence is apparent in this diagnosis, but, as Marney often said, there is more. Contradiction is joined with meaninglessness, uncertainty and a frantic search to fill our lives with activity:

The resultant "human situation" is a time out of joint. We become what we were never meant to be. No longer man— we are preoccupied, hurried, harassed. We are graspers, self-seekers, pushed by unworthy motives, based on unworthy hungers — no longer man. . . . Afraid of silence, we create a din. To avoid the threat of loneliness, we live in a crowd. Afraid of unemployment, we hire ourselves to death. Threatened by work, we become slaves to machinery. Aware of the dangers of isolation, we join everything. Shocked by old age, we camouflage with make up. Searching for rest, we drive ourselves to frenzy. . . Seeking relaxation, we come up with nerves. We write "Peace of Mind" and turn to suicide with an automatic. Uncertain of peace, we prepare for war.[15]

Marney saw modern men and women as especially susceptible to the seductions of materialism, provincialism, institutionalism and individualism. These forces are the "structures of prejudice," and he scrutinized them all in his volume by that title:

The first (materialism) is a metaphysical error, a perversion of reality; the second (provincialism) is an epistemological error, a false limitation of knowledge; the next (institutionalism) is the ethical error implicit in our

---

[14]*Faith in Conflict*, pp. 48-9.

[15]*Ibid.*, pp. 101-2.

satisfaction with lesser values; and the last (individualism) is theological madness, the denial of personality. Each participates in the rest, for few of our prejudices belong to one structure of culture alone; they combine in texture and strength to form a net, a cage, a cell—a padded cell![16]

The human tragedy, as Marney saw it, was not so much that in our early lives we have limited visions or perspectives, for this is inevitable. It is rather that we rest content with our lot, and are unwilling or unable to break out of the ethnic, national, social, racial, and economic frames which shape our consciousness. We are thereby limited in our perceptions and loyalties, molded by structures which unbalance us and create false centers of value. We fail to see that our institutions — clubs, committees, schools, churches, lodges, states, and nations — function as defenses against growth or vision. This propensity is not unique to America, of course; it is found in all cultures. In this ethos racism, nationalism, and religious institutionalism flourish. The consciousness of mass society, in Marney's view, is therefore inevitably a false consciousness; it perpetrates a bad faith and a trivialized Christianity. Marney observed:

> This superficial Christianity not only obscures our center of reference; it actively seeks to escape the possibility of being confronted by a valid center. Hence, superficial Christianity is everywhere an attempt to escape both Christ and the present moment in history. But superficial Christianity is clever. It will not admit to its attempt to escape Christ. It strives instead to escape the present, prattling about Christ all the while. . . .The real purpose is to escape the heavy demands of Christ in the present by seeking evening time before the morning's work is done.[17]

Not only in his books but also in his sermons and lectures Marney drilled hard on this theme. Wherever he looked, Marney saw people seduced by the sweet palliatives of denominations, inveigled by the myths of their culture, and subtly controlled by nationalistic propaganda.[18] Perhaps someone who lived in a less conventionally

---

[16]*Op. cit.,* p. 13.

[17]*Faith in Conflict,* pp. 105-6.

[18]In his unpublished diary of his Korean trip in 1954 Marney commented on the ambiguities between the need of a country to maintain armed forces (and to go to war

religious area of the country would have seen it differently; but in Austin and Charlotte, and the broader regions he reached through his travels, Marney clearly felt his task to be similar to Kierkegaard's: to help people become Christians when they think they already are Christians! *(Here is the task!)*

Marney's pastoral instincts, reflected in so many of his sermons and popular writings, kept him alert to other components of the human situation as well. Bewildering family dynamics, friendships which turn sour, loneliness, sickness, growing old, destitution, political betrayals, professional disappointments: all of these touched Marney's people and gave him (with Unamuno, whom he frequently quoted) a keen awareness of the tragic sense of life.[19] Marney was also sensitive to the fact that while he ministered to middle-class congregations with the luxury of middle-class dilemmas, other groups in society struggled for the very rudiments of life: food, clothing and shelter. In his formal writings, however, he addressed an educated, middle-class audience and focused on the contradictions in our personal lives and the demonic structures which corrupt our social awareness.

In theological method Marney followed Tillich and a tradition which goes back to Thomas Aquinas as he assumed (without question) the *analogia entis* — a connection between the state of humanity and the nature of the Divine. With Tillich, he also felt that any source which unlocks or clarifies the complexities of the human heart was a valuable source for theological thinking, hence his interest in Shaw's satirical jabs at piety, Goethe's grappling with evil in *Dr. Faustus,*[20] the contributions of novelists and anthropologists, and Freud's unmasking of the unconscious. He was, in this sense, a theologian of culture — not out of conviction that everything in culture can be revelatory of God, but in the sense that everything which lets us

---

when necessary) and the tendency of patriotic claims to be idolatrous. He was particularly sobered when one of the Protestant ministers selected by the Air Force was "bumped" from the mission at the last minute because a security check had revealed that he had on occasion preached sermons critical of the government. "On that score," he noted, "any one of us going on this trip could have been bumped."

[19]That theme is frequently dwelt upon in Marney's *Beggars in Velvet* (1960).

[20]It should be noted, however, that Marney had a dialectical sense of Goethe. He admired writings such as *Dr. Faustus,* but saw in Goethe the prototype of "rational" man who is no longer a model for the irrational, demonic forces of the twentieth century. See *The Recovery of the Person,* pp. 27-9.

understand the human condition without illusion is beneficial for clear theological thinking. During this period of Marney's career, *his anthropology is the clue to his theology.*[21] Reflecting on his fascination with the plight of humanity, Marney wrote:

> Is not all this to be explained by the fact that I am in love with man and mankind; that I see some basis for Feuerbach's contention that God is made in the image of man; that my preaching is filled with such anthropomorphic terms that I, too, run the risk of creating my God in the image of man I have loved? Is it not that I am a humanist and had best confess it? Is this embarrassment I have in claiming to know too much about God an honest rejection of temerity, or is it the background of a profound heresy with which I was inoculated in boyhood by men like Whitman, Voltaire, Clarence Darrow, H.L. Mencken, Sinclair Lewis, and the other iconoclasts who beat on my boyhood godhead until manhood became a substitute?[22]

Marney's sense of the contradictions and tragedies of life never caused him, however, to give up on humanity's potential. He understood Macneile Dixon's adopted motto QUI VITIA ODIT, HOMINES ODIT ("He who hates vice hates humanity"), but it is probably fairer to Marney to say that while hating certain deeds he always tried to care for the doer. An honest appraisal of the human predicament was the critical starting point for Marney's theology. His troubling realization that humanity, for all of its potential, could not heal itself, forced him to the question of God.

The Reality of God

During most of his Austin days Marney reflected a confidence in the reality and presence of the biblical God. His sermons, as one would expect, were biblically based and positively oriented. As all scholars know, an academic theologian can talk about "good news" when he feels like it. A clergyman has to talk about "good news" every Sunday at 11:00 a.m. whether he feels like it or not. There is no doubt that the responsibility of addressing congregations two or three times a week kept Marney engaged with the problem of the reality of God, and

---

[21]See *The Recovery of the Person*, p. 50.

[22]*Ibid.*, p. 35.

pressed him to speak when he often would have preferred to remain silent. Although he remained basically a theist, Marney felt the chilling winds of the modern intellectual climate assailing the biblical way of framing questions and of giving answers. Marney's concept of God shifted during the two decades we are considering in this chapter. His Austin sermons reflect more confidence in the biblical categories; his Charlotte sermons and lectures betray a struggle with the silence (or "eclipse") of God. We can perhaps best follow Marney's thought if we focus on two aspects: 1) the nature of God, and 2) our knowledge of God. Concerning the nature of God, let us initially consider two sermons from Marney's Austin days in the 1950's. I choose these sermons because they dealt directly with the concept of God; their emphasis, however, is consistent with almost all of Marney's preaching in that period and with the various sermons published in his first book, *These Things Remain* (1953).

The first sermon, entitled "God's Strong Hands," was preached in July of 1951 and was published independently by a group of friends of the First Baptist Church. In this sermon Marney stressed the personal, redemptive caring of God for all people. It is true that the life pilgrimage brings hurt, sorrow and brokenness to all of us—yet God has "strong hands" with which to carry our crosses. No matter how deep our hurt, how total our despair, how intense our self-hatred, God in His own way can and will fashion something good out of us. "God takes our sins and errors and turns them into victories." The Gospel, Marney maintained, reminds us to wait for God; briefly put, "a man must never let his disgust with the performance inveigle him into leaving before the play is over."[23] Our human tendency is to become so discouraged that we no longer believe that any person or power can redeem us. Judas did not wait for God, but God would have brought good even out of his defection. God's power never fails.

The second sermon, entitled "I Believe in God," was preached on September 27, 1953, and extended the theme of God as Redeemer into the broader processes of history. (We might note that this coincided with the emerging trend in biblical theology to speak of "God's mighty acts in history": God acting in Creation, Covenant, Christ, Church and Consummation to bring all things to redemption.) Yet Marney was cautious on this point. All the lessons of history are not so clear as one might wish nor as self-evident as some interpreters claim, and our

---

[23]*Op. cit.,* p. 15.

discernment of the plan and purposes of God is limited by our own backgrounds, culture, and intelligence. Nevertheless, eyes of faith can see the Spirit of God at work bringing healing not only to persons but also to nations. To make that clear is the task of prophetic preaching.

Several reflections are in order about these affirmations of God's nature. Marney's language here is more confessional than analytic; he proclaims rather than analyzes. He assumes the authority and validity of the biblical language about God. It is important to note that Marney never addressed the doctrine of God in a formal, academic way, even in his major book of this period, *Faith in Conflict.* When he spoke to groups of college students or to academic gatherings, Marney tended to move away from confessional proclamation to address more directly those facets of modern life which make belief in God difficult. A consideration of the bulk of his sermons and various lecture notes suggests, however, that Marney had a consistent sense of God's nature: God is personal, caring, and wills our wholeness. That is the good news of the Gospel.

The whole American theological climate shifted in the 1960's, however, and Marney felt the change. The old truism that in theology one generation's assumptions become the next generation's problems was vividly illustrated in the controversy over "God language." Marney's focus turned from the nature of God to the problem of our knowledge of God. He admitted his own quandary:

—(A) veteran of most of the classic descriptions of God, doctrines of God, dogmas about God; a reader of books on revelation, inspiration, the Holy Spirit, the Trinity, the Incarnation, I confess that I long for God, have waited for God and Godot, have run after God, have said more about God than I know; have worshipped God, felt for God, listened to God, analyzed God, prayed for God, to God, with God; and, like the rest of you, have beat on the gates of heaven when they were brass for some word from God to say.[24]

Such a note of uncertainty, however, is not the end of the matter. Marney held that even amid silence and mystery, none of us has been left alone by God. He believed that we know enough to be far better persons than we are, and that from the beginning "we have possessed

---

[24]*The Recovery of the Person,* p. 37.

more light than we have used." Even when our rational abilities fail us, or when mystical awareness is absent, or when calamities befall us, there is still a way of *obedience*. Too much intellectualizing about God, in fact, can be an escape from responsibility:

> I am saying, let us rest, for now, the doctrine of God in its present state of development. Let us turn to the consciousness that we have used the doctrine of God to keep from having to face the facts of man and mankind. There is no point in our continued praying to the Almighty to save a world he has commissioned *us* to save. The strength is in our hands. The knowledge is in our minds. We lack only the will to be and to do, and for these we can pray.[25]

Marney was not, however, as un-intellectual about our knowledge of God as the above quotation might suggest. He knew that the world of theological discourse revolved around several alternative ways of understanding the reality of God. He felt that liberal theology, in both its 19th and its 20th-century formulations, had serious shortcomings: too high a concept of man, too narrow a sense of the Kingdom of God, and too confident a sense of God's nature and presence. Marney likewise rejected Barth's counter-theme of God as TOTALITER ALITER, and instead insisted repeatedly that the only viable option for God-talk in our time was to speak of God as *Person*.[26] Critical to this understanding is the sense of God as "One who loves" — and who loves in a way analogous to our loving. (Marney responded deeply to Buber's concept of the divine "Thou.") Considering the classical theological dispute as to whether it is possible to speak of God as "needing" anything (and thereby implying an incompleteness in God), Marney insisted that it is no heresy to affirm that God needs the wholeness of humanity for his own satisfaction. God wills our well-being; in this way we are bound to God and the biblical concept of the covenant points to a profound reality.

To set Marney's affirmation of the reality of God against other theologians of his generation, he obviously shared Tillich's stress on the symbolic nature of all God language, but denied Tillich's insistence on a "God beyond the God of theism.' He was likewise unmoved by Tillich's symbolic term of "Being-Itself." Barth, on the other hand, was both too enamored with the Absoluteness of God and too confident in

---

[25]*Ibid.*, p. 38.

[26]*Ibid.*, p. 51.

the ability of words to describe the mystery of God. "Nobody *knows* fifteen hundred pages about God," Marney observed wryly, "even in German."[27] At this point in his career, Marney did not show much affinity for Teilhard's vision of the power who is controlling the biological, evolutionary processes of the physical world. Although he occasionally quoted Teilhard in sermons and lectures, he started at a different point in his own theology, and Teilhard's questions were not Marney's questions. Teilhard was fundamentally interested in the order of creation, and Marney in the nature of redemption.

Marney does show, however, a debt to Whitehead and the Whiteheadian tradition by describing God as a source of good, but not necessarily of all things. Marney never felt that God was the source of evil or tragedy. Any theological position which held that God is (a) the source of all that is and therefore (b) ultimately responsible for all of human tragedy as well as joy, struck Marney as nonsense. With Whitehead, Marney felt that it is far better to limit our sense of God's power than to posit the Divine as the source of evil.

One specific instance of this can be seen in Marney's understanding of nature. He took umbrage at theologians and poets who wrote odes to nature:

> Nature knows no anthems, no hymns, no religious nature songs which see God in birds and bees and sunsets and trees: when did nature change? There have been fifteen hundred floods on the Yellow River in the crowded canyons of China in three thousand years. The Yangtze has destroyed millions in regular floods. . . . Two hundred fifty thousand died last year of volcanoes, storms, freak winds, and nature's so-called acts of God. In what year did nature turn benevolent and begin to preserve for us the lie of a God of love? . . . reverence for life? Bah! What reverence can nature have for me—and even Schweitzer must destroy life to save for awhile another form of life. Nature is a world of ant warfare, bee executions, wolf raids and omnivorous plants. If God is love, it seldom shows in nature.[28]

When Marney speaks of God as Person, therefore, he is speaking of the source of love which can still be felt amid life's tragedies and

---

[27] *Ibid.*, p. 53.

[28] *Ibid.*, pp. 89-90.

sufferings. Without this trust—the courage to name the power which renews, forgives, sustains—life is absurd.

There are other roots to Marney's concept of God as well. Marney has his deepest affinities with those thinkers whom John Macquarrie has described as "Philosophers of Personal Being": Buber, Unamuno, Ortega, Berdyaev, and MacMurray. Macquarrie's judgment about this cluster of thinkers is likewise applicable to Marney: he calls them "prophets" rather than "philosophers," and suggests that within the broader intellectual ethos, they might aptly be called "seers," men of vision.[29] Thinkers of this stripe, he maintains, give us

> . . .illuminating insights into the genuinely human problems which concretely confront every one of us in the daily business of living....The great truth which these writers teach us is that we must take account of the personal realm, and that we cannot understand it in terms of anything but the personal itself, that is to say, in terms of our personal existence.[30]

That statement would also be a fair assessment of Marney's own position and intention.

Finally, our discussion of Marney's concept of God would not be complete without seeing Marney against the "Death-of-God" movement which flourished in the mid 1960's. Marney had a dialectical relationship to this movement. He obviously understood the impact of secularization upon the culture, and acknowledged what he called "a culture-wide loss of confidence, an endemic dissolution of an inner security."[31] He understood the world of the modern secular person which both Hamilton and Van Buren stressed so much. He knew that many persons — he himself, at times — experience a sense of void, loss, and emptiness whose reality is at the heart of the radical theology.[32] In a changing theological climate Marney did not defend old cosmologies, doctrines of creation or theodicies which he felt were better left behind. He considered them inessential for a vital sense of

---

[29]*Twentieth Century Religious Thought* (New York: Harper and Row, 1963), p. 207.

[30]*Ibid.*

[31]Mimeographed lecture, "The God of This Twilight," delivered at the Board meeting of the National Council of Churches, June 5, 1968, p. 2.

[32]See Marney's discussion of "The Eclipse of God" in *The Carpenter's Son.*

the Divine. For the most part, however, Marney felt that the radical theologies misplaced the emphasis. It is not so much that God has died, collapsed or failed; it is a human crisis: man, swollen with pride over his mastery of technology and things scientific, assumes that he is now "come of age." Yet, cautions Marney,

Man has not come of age

until he can accept the blame for his own situation;

until he can forswear his use of scapegoats;

until he can endure his own responsibleness;

until he can stand being so guilty;

until he can endure the history of his own mistakes.[33]

It is therefore personhood, not Godhood, which is at stake — and Marney was persuaded that a vision of the Transcendant Other is necessary for us to come to the fullness of personhood.

In a discussion with Thomas Altizer on Charlotte TV about the "Death-of-God" movement, Marney called it a "rub-a-dub-dub" phenomenon, and likened Altizer, William Hamilton and Paul Van Buren to "three men in a tub." On the contrary, said Marney,

. . . we are coming out into a wide and heaving sea that we do not know in the modern world, and I do not wish to go into it in a tub. I want a larger boat, and I am going to carry with me some sense of a Transcendent purpose, will and meaning. . . . I am looking for God and I intend to find him.[34]

It is beyond the scope of this study to trace the nuances of the Death-of-God theologies; the point here is to clarify that whereas Marney boldly faced the same questions, he offered a different answer, in large measure because he had already developed a more flexible, viable doctrine of God. On the God-problem—surely one of the most vexing in contemporary theology—Marney was more of a "soft" radical like

---

[33]"God of This Twilight," p. 2.

[34]Quoted by Robert Tabscott, "Memories of Marney," in *The Presbyterian Survey,* August, 1978, p. 10. It is worth noting that of the different viewpoints represented among the radical theologians of the late 1960's, Marney had no affinities with Altizer's Hegelian dialectics nor with Van Buren's linguistic analysis. He identified primarily with Hamilton's description of the 1960's as a time of the absence of God.

John A. T. Robinson than a "hard" radical like Hamilton, Altizer or Van Buren. The problem for him resided more in the inadequacy of historic Christian symbols than in the Reality to which the symbols point. *(w/ man's ability to understand God than w/ God Himself.)*

The Source of Redemption

Not surprisingly for a Christian pastor-theologian, Marney saw the clue to redemption, *i.e.* wholeness, in the Christ event. Although he allowed for a maximum of elasticity in interpreting the classical Christological terms, Marney saw them all as pointing to an event in which the deepest meaning of life is found. This focus on the Christ event dominates much of Marney's preaching in this period; it is found in his four small books of meditations—*He Became Like Us* (1964), *The Suffering Servant* (1965), *The Carpenter's Son (1967), and The Crucible of Redemption* (1968)—but was given its most sophisticated treatment in *The Recovery of the Person* (1963). As we shall see, Marney had alternative terminology for the process of redemption, which drew heavily upon the notion of personality, and how these two perspectives are related is not always clear. But let us turn initially to his Christology.

We might begin by noting that Marney owed more to the Pauline tradition than to the Synoptic Tradition: he was more drawn to the drama of Advent and Easter than to the words or deeds of Jesus recorded in the Synoptics.[35] Jesus is accordingly not so much teacher and herald as redeemer and revealer: God incarnate. Jesus was God *with a human face.* Marney leaned heavily on Irenaeus of Lyon as he struggled to make this point clear. He quotes Irenaeus:

> For He did not seem one thing while He was another . . . What He was, that He also appeared to be . . . not despising or evading any condition of humanity . . . . He caused human nature to cleave to and become one with God.[36]

Marney was not always happy with traditional Christian terminology, but he understood the wisdom of the early Church fathers who insisted that Jesus' humanity and divinity be bound together. At this stage in his career Marney had the same intent.

---

[35] *The Crucible of Redemption,* p. 8.

[36] Quoted in *The Recovery of the Person,* p. 95, and also in *He Became Like Us,* pp. 20-21. The quotation is from Irenaeus' *Adversus Haereses.*

Without a firm sense of Jesus' humanity—of his being like us—we lapse into Docetism. Without a sense of his divinity, there is no reason to call him "The Christ" and to proclaim his unique affinity with the Power which heals and restores. The clue for Marney was in the classical term *persona*, which then and now points to the Person of Christ:

> The Christian essential is the Person, Christ, who has as his aim to show the living God as his own to every individual. Christ is to history as the idea of God is to nature. He is even more conceptually real than historically real. He is not ever mere person but embodies a whole way of seeing the universe of God and man and our mutual relations. He is Christianity, and the God he reveals as center is anxious to draw us unto himself as the answer to evil.[37]

Marney was persuaded that the richness and significance of human personality had its genesis in God's incarnation in Jesus. Without this indwelling of God, the human species would be but another point on the continuum of living things. But the Christ event

> . . . is incarnation, which means of itself an interruption whether the world knows it or not. And here person, the quality of personalness, once more presses to the foreground. He identifies himself with human personalness in the same interrupting way that characterizes all incarnation. All birth of personality is incarnation.[38]

We must note in passing that Marney never wrote a scholarly book on Christology. He probably found the classic controversies too musty and the issues too academic to appeal to audiences struggling for meaning amid contemporary complexities. His interests as a pastor-theologian were different from those of academic theologians writing for scholarly debate. This point must be stressed because from a critical standpoint, Marney's approach to Christology is confessional, meditative, and poetic, not rigorous, analytical, or comparative. He deals with Christology en route to other issues, most specifically, what makes humanity fully human.

---

[37]*Faith in Conflict*, pp. 72-3. Marney found both Barth and Schleiermacher inadequate in their Christologies because they were reluctant to move from the person of the Christ to an affirmation of God as Person. See *The Recovery of the Person*, pp. 81-85.

[38]*Faith in Conflict*, p. 74.

When Marney considered the classic issue of the *work* of Jesus, he stressed the Cross. He rejected all notions of the Cross as ransom, substitution, or satisfaction, finding the assumptions behind those once-powerful theories inadequate for our day. Marney's theory of atonement rests primarily on his view of humans as deeply bound to the self and to this world: pride, the will-to-power and selfishness all reinforce our penchant for self-centeredness and false independence. What Jesus does on the Cross is to show us *how to deny ourselves*.[39] Only when we thus deny ourselves can we (like Jesus) know the "ultimate of otherness," a Thou-type relationship with God. To know ourselves as children of God therefore requires obedience, an act of will, a decision to claim a different way of being. There is nothing automatic about this new awareness of self; for the work of the Christ to be efficacious, it must be claimed existentially. Jesus must, Marney insisted, be Christ *for you*.[40]

With his flair for the dramatic, Marney often sketched out this scenario by saying that God is the actor, the Cross is the stage, the encounter between self and God is the situation, and our surrender to God is the denouement in this drama of redemption. Marney was ambiguous about the extent to which the person surrenders by will or is seized (or captured) by the divine initiative. With Augustine and Luther, he knew that both elements are present and important; but in the last analysis, Marney stressed the human decision: we choose to obey.

It is worth noting that Marney's Christology of this period had little, if any, resurrection emphasis in the classical sense. A close reading of his writing reveals an ambiguity on this point. What does the preaching of resurrection add to a Gospel that stresses obedience, an act of will, and the coming to true personhood? Is resurrection talk necessary, or is it a convenient way to talk about victory without sacrifice? Too often Marney saw it as a palliative, a repetition of fixed phrases, which mean nothing and change nothing.

To wrest some meaning out of "resurrection" Marney juxtaposed two viewpoints: the *objectivist* view (associated with biblical literalism, historic Roman Catholic and Anglican thought, and conservative Protestantism generally) that Jesus was raised physically from the dead and "objectively" wrought the redemption of the world;

---

[39] *Ibid.*, p. 77.

[40] *The Carpenter's Son*, p. 50.

and the *subjectivist* view (associated with Rudolph Bultmann) which holds that the history of the actual events of Jesus' life cannot be recovered, and that all Christian language about "resurrection" is mythic and symbolic. For Bultman the resurrection of Jesus becomes a meaningful assertion only when it symbolizes a shift from "death" to "life" in an individual believer. Marney felt that the modern discussion, as it moved between these two alternatives, overlooked the critical issue of the complexity of the person who is asked to decide on such a matter. As modern men and women we can hardly comprehend our *own* lives, let alone the history of Jesus or God's ultimate plan for history:

> I cannot even recover my own history. *I am a living myth:* images, masks, personages, interpretations, memories, drives, patterns and values so clutter my consciousness that at bottom I cannot know even one for sure. How can I expect to do more than bring these myths into orbit around a center?[41]

We might call Marney's alternative to the objectivist-subjectivist dichotomy a "personalist" view, thus linking it to the broader orientation of his theology. Clearly he repudiated all notions of resurrection which speak of a literal or physical raising of Jesus. He knew, with Bultmann, that if "resurrection" is to mean anything to modern men and women, its meaning must come out of their own lives. It testifies to a new understanding of the complex motives, drives, and dark recesses found in us all. Resurrection is a personal and not an objective truth; it is a confession of what has happened to us rather than what happened to Jesus. The proclamation of Jesus' "resurrection" is therefore only of value as a symbol for that which is possible in every person's life. It points to the genuine renewal that comes when we identify with Jesus' obedience, receptivity to God, and involvement with the plight of others. Marney was as leery of cheap resurrection talk as he was of cheap grace. He had heard too much talk in his time about objective, historical interpretations of Christ's triumph; for him all such language smacked of superficiality and hypocrisy:

> In all our world of Mecklenburg, and in Charlotte, the "city of churches," not one single, objective, historical church projection of the historical objective work and person of an

---

[41] *Recovery of the Person,* p. 103.

> objective historical Christ has truly taken hold of one single, powerful, effective, objective structure of evil to change anything. The gospel of the status quo is the only gospel we know.[42]

Only when we speak of "faith" in the active voice, only when we become new men and women can talk of "resurrection" be authentic.

Although Marney suggests that he is offering an alternative to the objectivist-Bultmannian controversy over the death and resurrection of Jesus, he in fact is much closer to the Bultmannian view than he acknowledges. His stress on finding the meaning of one's own history is basically the same as Bultmann's, albeit phrased in Marney's distinctive terminology. His only serious quarrel with Bultmann, as far as I can ascertain, is that he thought Bultmann talked too much about "history"and not enough about the person. A more careful reading of Bultmann might have allayed his concerns, for Bultmann was indeed concerned about the individual believer, but to pursue that point further is beyond the scope of this study.

In summarizing Marney's understanding of "resurrection" during most of his Austin and Charlotte days, it must be emphasized that Marney simply did not believe in the traditional interpretation of Jesus' resurrection. He was not sure it was a necessary theme; usually he found it more confusing than helpful. He could speak eloquently about incarnation, the Cross, faith, and obedience, and preferred to do so. When he did speak of resurrection, he did so in a Bultmannian sense and in that framework was convincing.

In a famous debate with Marney at Southern Methodist University, Albert Outler chided Marney for not taking the resurrection of Jesus more seriously, and predicted that some day he would do so. Marney replied, "If you're so smart, tell me when I'll do so." Outler answered, "You'll do so on the day you die." Those words haunted Marney; it is singular that during the last decade of his life, when his health failed and several times he was on the brink of death, he changed his mind about the meaning of resurrection. What that meant for him theologically we shall see in the next chapter.

The New Humanity

Those who surrender, those who take a new identity based on the

---

[42]*Ibid.*, p. 105.

Christ event, form the nucleus of the new humanity. It is this group which Marney felt could offer a hope for the transformation of culture. Several marks distinguish this new humanity (or "New Breed," as Marney liked to call them); one is the ability to recognize the power and omnipresence of corporate evil. Judgment comes, Marney insisted repeatedly, not only on us as individuals but on our corporations, institutions and value structures. Only when we accept responsibility for the culture we did not create are we able to repent for sins that we did not commit.[43]

Culture, of course, inculcates in us myths which distort our self-perceptions and our view of the human family: myths of race, class, ethnic origins, sex, religion, and economic order. Collectively they form, as we noted earlier, structures of prejudice. The new breed will be committed to break those structures by personal witness, political activism, and concerted opposition to the self-serving interests of privileged groups. Integrity and a clear vision of God will enable them to deal honestly and radically with prevailing myths:

> To be a person is to be able to share your myth—to share many sets of myths—to move freely in and out of living myths. To see life as religious, as feast, as celebration, as a dance of life and death, as myth, is to see it as it is. To be a person is to be able to move through the limitation of your own mythology to a larger one. To be a person is to be able to be open to the reading of your own discarded myths which leave their rings of skin and cartilage behind. To be a person is to be field of relation in relation with other fields of relation by way of myths held in common.[44]

As the above quotation implies, the deepest levels of personhood cannot be reached without a probing of our inward selves: a determined wrestling with motives, selfishness, and emotional complexities. Speaking to a meeting of the American Baptist Convention in Pittsburgh in 1967, Marney noted:

> This is what redemption is about. The redemption of my *humanum* is the acceptance of my source and limit. It is to know me, who I am; and the awful, primal, prowling powers that push little *Id* to make me serve the self. Unconsciously

---

[43]*Faith in Conflict*, p. 116.

[44]*Recovery of the Person*, p. 136.

there, deeply entwined with pious memories, I cannot face these primal powers of Original Sin alone. It takes a wife, or a brother, or some beloved, to midwife me on this labor. It's a journey to depth, never possible alone, never completed, always dangerous, and door-to-my-redemption: to fish that old cistern out and properly to label its old skeletons and carcasses of primal powers: lust, rapine, hate and greed. This *is* humanum.[45]

This courageous group of people will show marks of the secular world because they take it seriously and are engaged with it. They know, with Bonhoeffer, that the redress of the grave injustices of the past cannot be left solely in God's hands. They will take hold where they are: in large urban areas or in small towns, in ghettos or in suburbs, in churches and schools, in political movements and in professional fields. Theirs will be a vision rooted in the biblical symbol of "The Kingdom of God." They are marked by a strain of optimism about humanity's future. They will not be theologians in any traditional, academic sense but rather in a confident, active sense. Even as they sense the eclipse of God in our day they will pursue a better day for humanity with a sense of confidence:

> If we cannot see God or hear from God in our time, we will do his work in accordance with the *last* word we heard, and then, perchance, we may claim to have met him on the road from the job.[46]

The people of the new humanity will find strength in relationships. On this critical point Marney was indebted to Buber. He frequently cited two quotations from *I and Thou*: "In the beginning is relation," and "All real living is meeting." This community knows that we come to our deepest awarenesses through communion, dialogue, engagement. Marney was confident that a willingness to live life in this way would facilitate the breaking down of barriers which divide people. It would break down "role" barriers so deeply embedded in various vocations. A community of persons sharing a vision of a new humanity will honor all persons, not because of what they *do* but

---

[45]"The New Breed's Man" (published as a pamphlet by the Ministers and Missionaries Benefit Board of the American Baptist Convention, 1967), p. 7. (This lecture was slightly reworked and published as Chapter 19 of *The Coming Faith* in 1970.)

[46]*Ibid.*, p. 13.

because of who they *are*, and will be a place of depth, caring, and renewal.

Marney had a special interest in reviving the Reformation interest in "vocation." Properly understood, the term refers to more than a choice of a life work; it is a choice with an end in view. It is a "Calling":

> Vocation is the way one says *Thou* to God and all other thous. . . It receives its quality from the quality of its end— its God. It is the means by which the relation that is constitutive of persons is expressed. Vocation is the arena within which role, work and calling speak of the person who is becoming person—in terms of the quality of his relations with stuff, community, value and persons. Here vocation is redemptive, or it is not, in terms of persons and relations within these structures.[47]

Sensitive people who reflect on their vocations as instruments of service will be more effective agents of grace and ministers to the wider society. Marney liked to confront young people with this issue and to challenge young adults about the motives which had drawn them into different fields. Luther's long shadow across Marney's thought was instrumental in his development of the theme of vocation in his vision of the "New Humanity."[48]

The New Humanity and the Church

In his earlier years, including those of his ministry at Austin, Marney made distinctions akin to the classic themes of the "visible" and "invisible" church, while believing that the smaller nucleus who were genuine bearers of the Word was found within the ranks of the institutional churches. He was of course aware of the ambiguities of the Church as an institution, and some of his sharpest words in *Structures of Prejudice* were directed against the authoritarianism, bigotry, intolerance, reactionism, and provincialism of churches. The first word of the Church is consequently a word against bad religion, but at its best the Church attempts to be an instrument through which God's Spirit works for the Kingdom of God.[49] The Church has the

---

[47]*Structures of Prejudice*, p. 236.

[48]*Ibid.*, pp. 152-170.

[49]See Marney's lecture, "The Church: A Community of Witness," (mimeographed and undated). This lecture was apparently never published but was repeated by

Myers Park Baptist Church
Charlotte, N.C.

First Baptist Church
Austin, Texas

Marney at lecture.

Meyers Park Pulpit

Marney's mountain home, Wolf Pen Mountain, North Carolina.

Marney as Pastor
of First Baptist
Austin

Marney during his
days at the
Interpreter's House

Compassion
Gina Gilmour

potential for *koinonia* and *diakonia*; its members are in the process of becoming more aware of God, more ethical, moral, and personally sensitive. Marney felt that prophetic preaching could both illumine the blind spots of Christians and encourage the growth process.

Marney knew the Baptist tradition best, and recognized that one of its great needs was to identify with other streams of Christendom. A good example of how he undertook to stretch the thought of his people is seen in his sermon on "The World Council of Churches: Christ, Our Hope," preached in Austin on August 22, 1954, shortly after Marney had attended the World Council of Churches Assembly at Evanston, Illinois. He was moved by the ecumenical experience, urged his Baptist congregation to an "obligation of conversation" with all Christian bodies, and saw afresh in the Cross a symbol of the Church's stewardship to all the world.[50] Clearly during his Austin years he retained an optimism about the renewal of the churches and the promise of the ecumenical movement.

Marney's Charlotte years, however, saw much of that enthusiasm fade. The pervasive character of southern "culture religion" raised serious doubts about the amenability of the churches to genuine transformation. In 1963 he wrote:

> As for myself, I have less and less hope that denominational houses can offer any real redemption for us. Indeed, most times, as formerly, the institutional church seems somehow in the way. I look for, long for, some radical reconstitution, knowing all the time it will likely be preceded by an inevitable great turning away.[51]

In a sermon preached at Riverside Church in New York in 1964, Marney lamented that the Church is everywhere so afraid of change that it cannot deal with problems of poverty and the longing of the masses for a more just social order. The struggle for justice and the claims of all persons for a decent life, he observed, "are preached and fought on a different platform than the Church, except here and

---

Marney on several different occasions while speaking to groups of ministers in the 1950's.

[50]Marney subsequently indicated that he was the only Southern Baptist registered for the WCC Assembly. He was apparently invited because of his involvement with various ecumenical commissions of the National Council of Churches.

[51]*The Recovery of the Person,* pp. 100-101.

there."[52] Marney found more hope in "the Church at God's left hand": dedicated case workers, family counselors, nurses, teachers, fair employers—those who are in helping professions or who in any calling treat persons with dignity and fairness. It always sobered Marney to see that political, educational and even economic arenas of life showed more sensitivity to injustice and discrimination than did the churches. He knew that all Protestant churches needed more of God's Spirit, and a new vision of what they ought to be in a changing society.

Perhaps the clearest insights we have into Marney's changing ecclesiology of this period, however, are found in a series of lectures delivered from July 26-August 12, 1965, at a conference of ministers at Virginia Union University in Richmond. Here Marney began his move toward an ecclesiology of the world. Too long, he argued, the Church has been misled by a faulty doctrine of the Holy Spirit. We have wrongly assumed that the Spirit works primarily (or exclusively!) through the structures of the Church; this leads to a "cultural feudalism." When the Church is at its best it engages the world: it seeks to understand social, political, and economic complexities because it knows the corporate nature of both evil and grace. Let the Church be known for its ministry of mercy to all who are oppressed, for all people are God's sheep. Within this context, Marney called for inspirational liturgy, concrete preaching, and an openness to new theological categories. Effective witness amid a time of social revolution requires bolder ministers and a major reassessment of the Church's mission.[53] The angry critiques of American culture during this era from racial and student groups confirmed Marney's fears that the churches were, on the whole, bastions of reactionism; the question for him was whether a small cadre of concerned clergy and laity could be agents of renewal from within.

It gradually became apparent to Marney that a small group proclaiming an "Ecclesiology of the World" was not an adequate counterfoil to the weight of social conservatism in the churches. Towards the latter years of his Charlotte ministry, Marney was persuaded that the "invisible Church" may well dwell outside denominational sanctuaries. He had a growing appreciation for

---

[52]"Church and Race: A Never Ending Struggle," preached October 18, 1964, p. 4. This sermon, never published, was mimeographed and distributed by the Riverside Church.

[53]These lectures were never published; this summary comes from Marney's manuscripts in his files.

secular wellsprings of meaning and shared Michael Novak's view that
many non-Christians in America

> ... retain a profound conviction concerning the possibilities
> of intelligence in history, a fundamental and hopeful
> orientation toward a better future for man, a marked
> capacity to accept responsibility and to act, [and show] a
> profound respect for the human person and his freedom.[54]

It was thus that Marney began to appeal to a more diverse
audience. While insular, middle-class Christianity continued to gaze at
its own navel, Marney saw that the architects of a more human future
(trusting, of course, that one is possible) would come from diverse
religious, cultural and racial backgrounds. This idea, only a seed at this
point in Marney's career, sprang full-grown in the last decade of his
life.

Marney as Ethicist

Marney taught Ethics at Austin Presbyterian Seminary during his
tenure at The First Baptist Church in Austin, but that was an adjunct
appointment and his teaching duties had to be fitted into an already
heavy professional schedule. He was never an ethicist in the narrow,
academic sense of that term, but the demands of his preaching and
pastoral work forced him to deal constructively with contemporary
ethical issues. I reviewed several syllabi of ethics courses he taught at
the Seminary; they showed his thorough preparation in the history of
ethics and in the introduction to Christian ethics. He was obviously
familiar with the major thinkers of philosophical ethics—Aristotle,
Aquinas, Kant and Butler, to name but a few—and was likewise at
home with the leading thinkers and options in Christian decision
making. His lecture notes, all typed, were models of clarity and
organization. His major contribution to the intellectual life of the
Seminary, however, was his course in Social Ethics. There he drew
upon his first-hand familiarity with Texas politics to illumine for his
students the problems of Blacks, Chicanos, and poor people. His
classroom was a place of the "great awakening" for many white,
middle-class Presbyterian ministers of the southwest. James McCord,
who was President of Austin Seminary at that time, indicated that
Marney's work in Social Ethics was "electrifying." Marney, though a

---

[54]Quoted in "The New Breed's Man," *op. cit.,* p. 7. Novak's article is found in
Daedalus, 1967, p. 241.

part-time professor, was no amateur as a teacher or practitioner of Christian ethics.

Marney's most important contribution to the field of ethics was not, however, in the classroom. It was rather related to his work on the front lines of the ministry, when year in and year out he confronted pastoral tragedies, political ambiguities, social pressures and institutional demands. His audiences pressed him with the question of the "ought"—of action as well as belief. It is an old maxim in ethics that scholars can reserve judgment until all the data is in; people on the front lines have to make decisions at deadline time whether all the data is in or not. Marney's professional pace never allowed him the leisure for extended research into complex ethical theories, but he had a pastor's sharp instinct for ethical dilemmas. He understood the complaint of many pastors and lay people that the writings of academic ethicists are often too technical or antiseptic to be helpful. Marney never wrote a formal treatise on ethics, but ethical insights and convictions are woven throughout his sermons and writings. As one attempts to get a perspective on his interests and contributions to ethical analysis during his Austin and Charlotte years, five principles emerge which are helpful guides.

1. People are paramount. As we have already noted, Marney began with the assertion of a personal God. Concomitantly he emphasized the personhood of Jesus and the distinctiveness of every human being. People are always more important than divine ordinances. Marney was chary of any approach to ethics which argued that God's purposes can be clearly known and fairly proscribed for all human situations. The human situation is too ambiguous, and our moral circumstances too complex, for a legalistic ethic to be adequate. As a pastor Marney saw the tragedy which befell people when they were judged or treated by inflexible moral maxims . Ethical absolutism was of the same order as theological dogmatism. His basic interest was in personal wholeness; his approach to persons and problems was therefore situational and pragmatic. Marney had more in common with situation ethicists than with deontologists (i.e., ethics based on "divine commandments") or natural law proponents. Love (he was uneasy about attempts to define different types of love, such as Anders Nygrens's classic distinction between "agape" and "eros") [55] is the critical ingredient which restores, renews and redeems human life, and

---

[55] _The Recovery of the Person,_ p. 55.

what love entails must be judged by a thoughtful assessment of circumstances.

Marney was enough of a Niebuhrian, however, to know that even a personalist ethic could not be based solely on the principle of love. The pervasiveness of corporate evil (noted earlier in our theological discussion) means that an ethicist must be concerned about social structures and the struggle for justice. Love heals human hearts; justice (always imperfect) rectifies social inequities; people are molded by both arenas of existence. A pastor-theologian responds to both types of hurts: never as academic or theoretical problems, but with the specific needs of persons in mind. Marney differed from most of the situation ethicists in his persistent concern for the corporate structures which shape the whole fabric of society. On the whole, Marney was prophetic and critical when dealing with social structures and grace-oriented when dealing with people.

Marney transcended the controversy between "self-denial" and "self-fulfillment" which has recently drawn so much attention in Christian ethics. Basically his sermons and lectures consistently asserted that in our self-denial (obedience, the act of will) we come to find our true fulfillment. He frequently quoted the text of Jesus, "Whoever would save his life will lose it, and whoever loses his life for my sake will find it." (Matt. 16:25, RSV).

By any criteria, however, Marney insisted that Christian ethics must keep the *person* in central view—not rules, maxims, absolutes, nor sagacious theories of past thinkers.

An example of this ethical stance can be seen in Marney's essay on "The Christian Community and the Homosexual," originally published in *Religion in Life* and subsequently reprinted in various anthologies of ethical writings.[56] Rejecting the view of homosexuality as a biological abnormality, Marney (following Freud and Menninger) saw its roots in a retarded emotional development and in cultural repression. He was appalled at historic Jewish and Christian approaches to the "problem" (noting the heinous punishments prescribed in the *Mishnah*), and deplored the wooden, inadequate

---

[56]"The Christian Community and the Homosexual," in *Religion and Life,* Winter, 1966. Reprinted in *Moral Issues and Christian Response,* edited by P. Jersild and D. Johnson (New York: Holt, Rinehart and Winston, Inc., 1971).

approaches found in Karl Barth and Helmut Thielicke.[57] He particularly faulted Thielicke for failing to grasp the fundamental androgyny of every person, a failure which led Thielicke to posit a sharp duality between male and female and to assume a clear male and female "norm" from which the homosexual deviates.

Marney maintained that the repression of the homosexual (in the culture and in the Church) results from a combination of hysteria, social conditioning and ideological bias. The Church's error lies 1) in its inability to collectively acknowledge its own failure in dealing with the sexual complexities of people; 2) in its inadequate expression of community, so that class, race and sexual diversity still divide congregations; and 3) in its failure to probe more deeply the relationship between grace and sexuality—under what circumstances does sexuality convey grace, and when does it not? In Marney's view, Christians should more appropriately be concerned about aggression, exploitation, and psychic injury of others, whether such acts are committed by homosexuals or heterosexuals. An obsessive and pernicious concern with homosexuals often obscures the suffering found in many heterosexual relationships and denies the guilt which we all bear. We *all* lack the ability to love. What is needed is for the Church to speak with a sane voice, and be a community of compassion and grace, for all who struggle to find love and dignity in their sexual lives. We do not honor our Lord, said Marney, when we stereotype people, condemn them without knowing who they are, and isolate them from the bonds of community.

There is more to be said about the handling of this complex problem by the Christian community, of course; the point here is merely to illustrate how Marney ruled out stereotyping and judging by "divine" norms in his ethical considerations. He knew enough about anthropology and sociology to understand the phenomenon of social conditioning, and in all matters he sought to hold paramount the place of the individual.

2. *There are no "sanctified" people.* In this assumption Marney stands with Luther and Reinhold Niebuhr against Calvin, Wesley and Jonathan Edwards. Confusion, hypocrisy, greed, and selfishness are with us all the days of our lives, and masks of deception are not

---

[57]Barth's views are found in the *Church Dogmatics,* Vol. III, Part II, (iv); Thielicke's position is delineated in his well known *The Ethics of Sex* (Cambridge: J. Clarke, 1964).

removed even after a visit by the Holy Spirit. The "redeemed" person (as Luther said) is redeemed from Sin but not from sinning. Confidence in life comes not through claiming goodness for ourselves but in trusting in the renewing, forgiving grace of God.

Marney knew that to *know* the right and to *do* the right are two different matters. It is indeed possible to think clearly and to *do* nothing at all (a major tendency in academe, he noted).[58] Ambiguity clouds our situations and our perception of alternatives. The hope for a higher level of life Marney found in the *will*: the person as a decider, "who must either look toward the Other or turn his head."[59] That choice should be the focal point of Christian teaching and preaching. To do the right is such a struggle, however, that often the power to act must come through the "invasion" of our wills by the Other. Marney thus bypassed the classic divide between roles of the will and divine grace in decision-making, insisting instead on a synergistic relationship.

To say that there are no sanctified people is not to say that all people are equally bad, or that there are not momentous choices which we all have to make in the course of the human pilgrimage. What Marney objected to most strenuously was the notion of a two-tiered humanity: the saved and the damned, the righteous and the unrighteous, saints and sinners. On this point Freud corrects Christian piety. No Christian decision or experience renders one immune from the temptations and confusions which are a part of the human condition. "The war is won," he once observed, "but the battle is not done."[60]

This conviction gave Marney a realistic sense of the Church and an instinctive dislike for displays of piety. Those who knew him knew that too much religiosity caused him to chafe and mumble epithets. He frequently commented that (like Bonhoeffer) he was more attracted to secular than to religiously-oriented people. What he admired most were people who lived without pretense. Marney found much in conventional middle-class Christianity that leads to conformity, prudery, loss of nerve and courage. By contrast, he felt that Christian faith should lead to confidence, humor, audacity, honesty, and

---

[58] *Recovery of the Person,* p. 29.

[59] *Ibid.,* p. 147.

[60] *Faith in Conflict,* p. 79.

imagination. Seeing a world faced with massive problems and a Church in need of *real* men and women, Marney once observed that dealing with trivial problems of middle-class people was like "being stoned to death by popcorn." Luther's earthy realism and his call to "sin boldly" echoed through Marney's vision of the Christian community.

3. *Values are molded by ideologies.* This is the implicit message of Marney's *Structures of Prejudice,* which in 1961 was far ahead of the ethical reflections of that time. Marney analyzed materialism, provincialism, institutionalism, and individualism, looking at how they shaped the mentalities of classes, ethnic communities, religious groups, and nations. He did not cast his analysis in the precise language of today's discussion of ideology, but his instincts were similar. He saw that privileged groups develop rationales to justify the status quo and their place in it. He knew that nations will always act in what they deem to be their own self-interest and that in times of political crisis nationalistic appeals always skirt dangerously close to idolatry. He recognized the pervasive nature of racism and the natural tendency toward exploitation of the weak. He looked disdainfully on philosophical and psychological viewpoints which absolve people of responsibility for their fellow human beings. We are all implicated by the presence of deceit, fraud and narcissistic self-interest. "Realism"— the Reinhold Niebuhr variety—was therefore a *sine qua non* for Marney in ethical analysis.

As perceptive as Marney was about ideology, it is surprising that he did not pursue the application of these insights to an analysis of the place of white males in western culture. No theologians of the period, however, foresaw the development of liberation theology and its critique of the sexist and class assumptions of our culture.

Marney did not allow his awareness of ideology to lead him to repudiate social structures or the legitimate functions of government. It is wisdom, as he once said in a sermon, to know that we are molded by social structures; it is madness to assume that we can live without such structures. The social fabric of community and the pervasiveness of evil in the world mean that nations have to have military strength and the capacity for self-defense. There are legitimate social programs of the government to redress broad scale problems: for this reason Marney supported the TVA, civil rights legislation, and the Johnson administration's war on poverty. Ethical realism enables one to see through mythologies. It does not lead to despair, withdrawal, or nihilism. It facilitates, rather than negates, responsible involvement in politics.

4. The ambiguities of politics. Politics, noted Marney more than once, is finally about power—and power inevitably corrupts and dehumanizes those who have it.[61] Politics is a necessary component of society, but the political process is approximate, tentative and unjust. Politics alone cannot redeem the social order. Christians should be seriously engaged in political causes but cautious about identifying them with the Gospel or being utopian in their expectations. The real nature of politics, Marney felt, was described most lucidly by Niccolo Machiavelli in his works *The Prince* and *The Discourses.* Machiavelli, Marney maintained, was not trying to write essays on the morality of politics; he was simply attempting (we might say) "to tell it like it is" in the political sphere. Machiavelli's various suggestions to would-be rulers—e.g., not to worry about conventional morality, that it is better to be feared than loved, that one can destroy opponents by accusation, that one rules best by coercion—these Marney saw as clues to the nature of politics.[62]

Marney preached these themes to his prominent political constituency in Austin and to activist-inclined young people on campuses around the country. His perceptions were undoubtedly influential in his personal decision to keep some distance from the political activists of the 1960's who felt that they could initiate a transformation of the country through political processes. For Marney, some political sensitivity was essential but too much hope for politics is folly. His ethical realism served as a corrective to the utopianism of radical politics.

5. The value of the indicative. Much of Marney's effectiveness as a preacher and lecturer was in his tendency to speak in the indicative mood. He had a gift for seeing visions, conceiving possibilities, and clarifying theological principles for his audiences, without tying them to specific strategies for implementation. He liked to talk about planting seeds in the human conscience, where they could develop as they would. Marney of course drew some criticism from friends and colleagues for the approach; some even accused him of "being long on

---

[61]*Structures of Prejudice*, p. 209.

[62]Marney first developed his analysis of Machiavelli in a series of radio talks in Austin. A more condensed version is found in *Structures of Prejudice*, pp. 210-15.

parables and platitudes." This was, however, a deliberate posture on his part, and was consistent with his concept of the person. He knew that people do not respond to being shamed, embarrassed or condemned; they change their attitudes and involvements because they have seen or heard something higher. Marney felt that this was true of people in their personal lives as well as in their approach to social issues. At the personal level it mitigates against defensiveness and guilt; at the social level it allows for a healthy diversity in political outlook. As Marney used this approach to the social arena, he was quite close to William Temple's orientation in his well-known volume *Christianity and Social Order*.[63] Temple argued there that theological convictions give the Christian a vision for the social order but do not prescribe specific strategies to be universally adapted. Marney, like Temple, was more interested in clarifying the *ends* rather than the *means* of a more Christian society.

Inasmuch as Marney's two prominent congregations were both more intrinsically conservative than Marney, this style undoubtedly was necessary to Marney's effectiveness as a pastor-theologian. It should be said, however, that this approach was for Marney not just a means of survival in hostile climates, but a basic conviction about the best way to move from the realm of ethics to the realm of morality.

Summary

We have attempted in this chapter to clarify the main themes of Marney's theology during the two decades of his career when he was a pastor-theologian of national visibility. We have noted that Marney drew upon a wide range of other thinkers—theological and humanistic—but gave a distinctive twist to his sources as he adapted them to his southern audiences. In his affirmation of God, he is distinctive in his stress on God's love and grace at the expense of God's omnipotence and omniscience. These latter characteristics, I suspect Marney would say, are aspects of God about which we cannot know, and discussion about them is finally academic and perhaps irrelevant. The mystery of creation is solved through scientific research and not by dogmatic assertions. Not being a systematic theologian, Marney never had to put into print his reservations concerning the doctrine of creation; from a Christian standpoint he simply felt it was adequate if one could genuinely hold to a doctrine of redemption. At a conference

---

[63]London: Penguin Books, 1942.

at Union Theological Seminary in New York in 1961, I heard someone ask Marney what he thought the space age did to the doctrine of creation. Marney replied that it made the doctrine look like "a parasite on a grapefruit rind going down a sewer." As long as we are persuaded of grace, however, there is a valid Christian gospel!

We noted how Marney stressed the Cross in his Christology far more than the resurrection. He sensed that the traditional resurrection accounts were more problematical than helpful, and furthermore were not essential to the deepest meaning of the gospel. To encounter the Cross of Christ as that which pierces our personal myths and masks and brings us to a fresh awareness of our potential as children of God: that is miracle enough.

Marney's search for a "new breed" of person, his struggle to renew and revitalize his congregation, his skeptical attitude toward religious bureaucracies, his suspicion of piety, and his distrust of politics were all part of a personal way of being as well as of a theological position. Although he did not have the analytical gifts of a Reinhold Niebuhr or Paul Tillich, he was able to creatively synthesize and apply persuasive theological insights. He spoke and wrote with a poetic flair and compelling candor; those who knew him best often felt that he had to be *heard* to be appreciated. He was the message.

Marney's convictions and style as developed in these years were not the last step, however, in the pilgrimage of this Southern viator. New priorities and theological convictions emerged as he left the pastorate for his final sojourn at the Interpreter's House. It is to that phase of Marney's life that we now must turn.

CHAPTER IV

MARNEY AS CHRISTIAN HUMANIST

"Mercy heals in every way. It heals bodies, spirits, society and history. It is the only force that can truly heal and save."

—Thomas Merton, *Love and Living*
(London: Sheldon Press, 1979), p. 216.

"What if Jesus Christ is more question than answer? And what if the question is man?"

—Marney

The time span we are considering in this chapter (1967-78) covers the last eleven years of Marney's life. It is the period of his ministry at the Interpreter's House. The emotional, professional and personal transitions involved in his move from Charlotte have already been noted and do not need to be recapitulated here. Into this strange new setting Marney brought his abundant strengths: his charisma, his personal ties throughout the South, and crucial contacts with denominations and foundations which helped the Interpreter's House get launched. His new responsibilities, as well as the changing cultural context of America in that period of time, led him to new sources of thought and prompted him to dig more deeply into old sources.

Marney's professional interests during this period were twofold. First, in his work at the Interpreter's House, he developed his interests in the psychology of personality. In this arena, he drew primarily on Ruel Howe, Robert Raines, Hobart Mowrer, Paul Tournier, Abraham Maslow, Denis de Rougemont and Karl Menninger. Methods of self analysis, group dynamics, and the processes of healing became more central to his work than ever before, and his own skills as a pastor were deepened. These interests were more intense for Marney in the earlier years at the Interpreter's House than in his later years, but for a time they constituted a genuine refocusing of his professional endeavors. Detailed consideration of the manner and method of Marney's personal ministry at the Interpreter's House lies beyond the scope of this study, but we shall attempt to show in this chapter how these psychological humanists influenced the broader range of his theological endeavors.

Secondly, Marney continued to wrestle with the ambiguities of the Church as institution and the quandaries of the professional ministry. On these fronts, we can discern a continuity with lines of thought articulated at Myers Park, but new interests in natural theology, in the Jewish foundations of Christianity, and in the *gestalt* of the theology of the Apostle Paul emerged as well. Behind these broader explorations lies the influence of Teilhard de Chardin, whose final evolutionary vision attracted Marney (though Marney found him a "bit romantic"). Marney once noted that Teilhard "moved me as no other Catholic writer of our time."[1] Michael Polanyi also entered Marney's field of vision, not only for his work in epistemology which sought to transcend the old split between scientific and humanistic modes of knowing, but also for his conviction that purposive life requires a commitment to some vision higher than the individual.[2] Abraham Maslow's work on human advancement was supportive of Marney's insistence that we can work for a better society without becoming quixotic or utopian. Surprisingly, however, and perhaps most importantly for Marney's new ventures in theology, we see him returning to the theological vision of Paul of Tarsus, utilizing Paul as a source for a radical vision of Christianity. That vision was pivotal for the last decade of Marney's life and is the over-arching principle around which most of his other ideas have to be seen. What was this radical idea?

---

[1] *Priests to Each Other* (Valley Forge, Pa: Judson Press, 1974), p. 106.

[2] See *The Coming Faith*, pp. 122-4. There is no evidence to suggest, however, that Marney pursued Polanyi's thought beyond Polanyi's *Personal Knowledge* (Chicago: University of Chicago Press, 1958).

The New Vision: A Universal Humanism

In a theological landscape already shaken by Bonhoeffer, John A.T. Robinson, the Death-of-God movement, scientific discoveries, secularism, and the crumbling of old parochial barriers, Marney knew that the foundations of Christendom were shifting. Something was in the *Zeitgeist* waiting to be born. Marney thought that our time might even be compared to the first century or to the times of Luther. What is it that is emerging? Marney noted:

> I do not know except that it is something about man so great we have never believed or received it. Something about man that makes all our localisms, regionalisms and nationalisms subject to constant revision. It is something about man so great as to turn all our lesser loyalties into damnable perversions when they get in its way.[3]

The clue for this new idea, Marney felt, was in seeing the Apostle Paul as one who shifted the focus of God's concern from the parochial to the universal: as one who saw that the real import of the Christ revelation was that God has received all the nations, and that the road to personhood is open to all. We have then, in the thought of this first great Christian interpreter, a vision of "The New Human Race." Marney mourned that with so many studies of Paul over the years, we have lost sight of this one major revolutionary concept!

To support his interpretation of Paul's vision, Marney cited Barth's exegesis of Paul (especially on Romans 5) as Barth deals with this text in *Christ and Adam, The Humanity of God,* and Volumes IV (1) and V of the *Dogmatics.* What intrigues Marney most, of course, is Barth's insistence on Paul's universalism: what is Christian is fundamentally universal, and nothing in human nature is alien to Christianity. The theological implications are staggering because they go so much against the grain of our carefully developed western theological systems. The real truth of the gospel is that "God intends all things unto himself so fully that we co-work with God whether we know it or not."[4] Can we stand such knowledge? What will it do to us?

Basically, once we see the vision, argued Marney, we can live with a sense of confidence. We no longer have to bear all the burdens of our own histories. We can accept ourselves and know that it is all right to

---

[3] *The Coming Faith,* p. 38.
[4] *Ibid.,* p. 57.

be who we are. Likewise we are relieved from instinctual hostilities towards others: we can enjoy them, celebrate with them, because we know we share a common humanity. As Christians we can be—indeed, must be—opened to the whole world, for indeed:

> "There is neither Jew nor Greek, slave nor free, male nor female —for we are all one in Christ Jesus" (cf. Gal. 3:28)

To believe this is to refuse to accept the divisions of class, race, sex, rank, orders of holiness, levels of piety, ethnicity, and regionalism. Old in its roots, this message is radical in its impact. Marney concluded:

> The Coming Faith is a Judeo-Christian based Universalism. For awhile we shall cling to our adjectives such as Judaic, or Christian, or Protestant, or Catholic—but they are all adjectives among other precious adjectives. That is to say, the new noun is *man*. The new dimension is a *humanism*. There is no humanism that is not also a *universalism*, even if you still insist upon calling it a *Christian* universalism.[5]

This was the *cantus firmus* which underlay almost all of Marney's theological endeavors in his last decade. It marked a transition from a *Weltanschauung* rooted in the Christian tradition to a broader, inter-faith, inter-cultural perspective. "I have known for years," Marney observed in 1974, "that our future must feature a broader ecumenism than any Christian expression can contain."[6] There was something powerful to Marney in the realization that faith need not separate its followers from other believers or from non-believers. A universal humanism reveals and deepens our ties with the whole human family. Perhaps naively, but certainly optimistically, Marney felt that if this vision could be grasped it would be the basis for a new age. "It would stop all religious wars in our future if we knew this simple fact—*all Religion is One*."[7]

Marney's intent here is subject to misunderstanding and must be clarified. He does not seek a homogeneity of the world's religions. He

---

[5] *Ibid.*, p. 80

[6] "Beyond Our Time and Place" (The Dickson Lectures at Myers Park Baptist Church in 1974), p. 47. This series of lectures was apparently printed privately by the Church, and Marney's four lectures appear to have been included in a larger volume. I came across these lectures in Marney's files; this quotation comes from the first lecture, entitled "Hail and Farewell."

[7] *Ibid.*, p. 50.

is not calling for a world devoid of particularity, custom, and tradition in its religious forms. He rather insists that the term "God" means the "Oneness of things." It means that all things are holy. There are no legitimate distinctions between sacred and secular; no independent realm of the Divine and the human. It means to see, with Teilhard, that "the whole cosmic process is Sacramental," and that there is, in the very heart of things, a repeated cycle of sacrifice and survival. The person who can embrace a universal humanism will honor all those religious traditions which point in awe to the Divine and esteem the worth of persons. We can continue to wear our denominational labels (not for theological significance but perhaps for social convenience), but a humanist-oriented faith "would certainly mean the death of all our stupid exclusive claims, and the death of all our stupid superiority debates, and the end of all our estrangedness."[8]

The discerning reader will note that this concept of a universal humanism has some affinities with Marney's call for a "New Breed" of person discussed in Chapter III. The basic characteristic of the "New Breed," however, was a coming to personal wholeness and authenticity. The *journey inward* enables a person to then see new things as he/she looks outwards. The emphasis was on the renewal possibilities of this group as leaven in the human loaf. Now, however, Marney has shifted the focus. The clue is a theological insight about the oneness of the human family: the vision is broader and includes all of creation. A universal humanism includes all that Marney had said about his hopes for a new type of "holy" person and goes beyond it.

Theological Foundations for Christian Humanism: Judaism

Although in his volume *The Coming Faith* Marney based this new vision on an exegesis of Paul, he clearly found another starting point in the faith of Judaism. He developed these ideas in a sermon preached in 1969 at Riverside Church in New York on the occasion of Ernest Campbell's installation as Senior Pastor.[9] One of the greatest tragedies of Christian history, he insisted, has been our repudiation of Judaism. We rejected our roots by denying the profound insights of that tradition. Against Barth, who said that Judaism is a "temptation" for Protestantism, Marney insisted that to know the faith of Judaism is an *opportunity*. Judaism holds for us, as it did for Jesus, "fountains of

---

[8]*Ibid.,* p. 52.

[9]"Toward Judah," *The Christian Century,* October 22, 1969, pp. 1345-48.

living water." In times when theologically we hardly know how to speak, Judaism reminds us of "a righteousness between man and creation."[10] Judaism points us toward an involvement in the world; toward a realistic and hopeful concern for the human future; toward a healthy sexuality, and to a faith posture which doesn't have to lie by claiming to know more than it knows.

Not only the faith of Judaism—which above all has affirmed human dignity and integrity—but also the symbols of Judaism are rich for those who seek a universal humanism. Jerusalem, the place of memory and future gathering; Shabbat, the day of celebration; wine and bread, reminders of the good earth and of human sustenance: these universalize and sanctify our daily lives. When we are bewildered in the face of complexity or silenced by the paucity of our own experience, Marney felt that the source of renewal could be found in the fountains which nourished Jesus.

Marney, we might note, had had a deep respect for Judaism all during his ministry. He recalled once that he had received over 800 letters of protest when he began his 1965 Christmas Day sermon at Myers Park (entitled "Peace But Not Yet" and televised nationally by CBS) with the Jewish Shema. He preached repeatedly in his pastoral days from Old Testament passages and loved to exegete the Hebrew text. In 1974 he spoke with obvious approval of a fellow Protestant clergyman who had decided that of all possible religious labels the most appropriate one for him was "Reform Jew." As Marney summarized in his Riverside sermon: "Atonement for crimes, balm for wounds, recovery from illusions—they lie toward Judah."[11]

The New Humanism and Old Theological Categories

Since he was usually interpreting his vision of universal humanism to Christian audiences, Marney tooks pains to show that this is a valid way of understanding the Gospel and not a new heresy bred in the western North Carolina mountains. He consequently employed traditional theological terms but in fresh, distinctive ways. (He obviously learned much from Tillich on that score!) One such term was "incarnation"—a term so pregnant with meaning for traditional Christianity that many have asserted that it is the critical word in the whole Christian vocabulary. Marney used the word frequently, but

---

[10]*Ibid.,* p. 1347.

[11]*Ibid.,* p. 1348.

interpreted it to mean something other than God "taking human form."

In *The Coming Faith*, for example, where Marney is primarily concerned to exegete Paul, he draws on musical imagery, suggesting that in passages such as Philippians 2:5-11 (where Jesus is said to have "emptied himself, taking human form") Paul is basically writing a cantata. Paul's language, Marney says, is a way of describing "a brightness and intensity of relation to the Father that he had never known by way of the beloved Law."[12] The term "Christ" refers to the Spirit which now embraces all nations for all time. The name embodies the new vision of universalism:

> His universalism, his escape from the parochialism of Judah
> into the oneness of mankind has a proper label. His move
> from one ghetto into a New Human Race bears the name of
> the Lord of the Race—Lord by virtue of his primacy. He,
> the first to make it to a proper manhood—is exalted, and
> here we bow . . . and hence, all are called.[13]

"Incarnation" thus is not to be taken literally but symbolically. It does not refer to a God who walked on earth in human form, but rather to the uniqueness of one who showed us our true destiny as persons—our "proper manhood."

In other lectures and essays, Marney quoted H.H. Farmer approvingly that "the central essence of the Christian faith is...belief in the incarnation."[14] The enthusiasm with which he could make such statements led him to sound orthodox enough, but Marney's intent was clearly to put new wine into this old wineskin. He noted that the idea of incarnation of a deity is not unique to Christianity; it has parallels in many other religious movements in the Greco-Roman world. Two special emphases in the Prologue of John's Gospel, however, clarify the distinctiveness of the Christian claim: 1) that in Jesus we can *identify* the true essence of God, and 2) that in Jesus it became clear that God "takes up his abode in us." At this moment of history something new entered human consciousness: a social concern, a writhing of the spirit, a restlessness with the way things are, an alternate vision for the human family. Having discovered the essence

---

[12]*The Coming Faith*, p. 91.

[13]*Ibid.,* p. 93.

[14]"The Language of Revelation," N. D. (a mimeographed lecture from the Interpreter's House), p. 3.

of God, we were invited to share in a new way of being: "To everyone who took him in once for all, in them did he for all release the power to be an Incarnation too."[15] Jesus' uniqueness, in other words, was in degree rather than in kind. With trust in the validity of what he made known, we, too, can come to our full destiny as persons.

Marney's assumptions and theological orientation require explication on this point. Earlier in this study we noted that for Marney all theological language is symbolic. In a Tillichian sense, language is instrumental; as symbols, terms participate in that to which they point. Underlying our theological language is our experience, and Marney holds that Paul's language is rich because it captures Paul's experience of initiation into a new humanity. "Christ" is a name for that which is greater than a name: the term participates in, but is not the whole of, reality. And what should we do, as we seek to share in Paul's experience? Have the *mind of Christ* in us (Phil. 2:5). We can use the name of Christ, and share the Spirit of Christ, because in that name we have a new sense of who God is, who we are, and who our neighbors are. For Marney, this celebration is better expressed in a musical, rather than a verbal, idiom.

This illumines how Marney could utilize the *logos* language of the Fourth Gospel but also have a particular understanding of what it meant. Jesus is not God incarnate in some literal sense. He was not a divine being on this earth. He was a Jew, nourished in the faith of Judaism, who knew God as Father, and who taught us that God cares utterly for us. The man Jesus was an instrument through whom God acted to show that He identifies with our sufferings and that "our suffering belongs to sense and meaning."[16] It is in this sense he can be called "the Christ." The point is that although Marney could wax eloquent on "incarnation," in classical categories he had a "low" Christology: Jesus was one through whom God worked. In his Preface to *The Coming Faith*, Marney wrote:

> I plead also for a renunciation of that fundamental heresy that Jesus is God. This keeps millions from loyalty to our banners. To call Jesus God is an impertinence against Christ and God. For the Son is not the Father. He is son, and man-son at that. And I hope for the Jewish hope to be

---

[15]*Ibid.*, p. 5.

[16]*Priests to Each Other*, p. 46.

rediscovered. That hope that knew about a Father.[17]

Closely related to such an understanding of incarnation is the term "revelation." What does God reveal? Again Marney could offer a conventional definition: "Revelation means the peculiar activity of God in the unveiling of his hiddenness."[18] Marney ties this idea to the notion of universal humanity by probing the *means* and *process* of revelation. God's revelation comes to us not as static possession but rather as a continuous event. It inaugurates a "continuing conversion," as each new day brings new awareness of how we are bound to our culture, assumptions and myths: *(in faithing") ("Christing")*

> This is the language of revelation: When you are in the processes of change, under a judging loving demand, that makes you stand for some things and against others; when in your relations you are aware of an Other reaching for you; when you are being filled and used and committed to new ends, with the old slipping away; when the One who is no longer your sure possession becomes your companion in a conversion and revolution; you are under revelation."[19]

Marney furthermore was not convinced that we can, or should, speak of Jesus Christ as a "final" revelation of God. Perhaps, he mused, we are just now at the beginning point of understanding what God asks of us. One thing is sure: God's revelation has nothing to do with dogma or propositions. It has everything to do with persons, relationships, caring, and ministering to the hurts that are around us. Revelation opens us outwards. Revelation from God, Marney maintained, is always local and personal. It moves us to do something where we are. We could even say that to be a recipient of revelation means "to put one's resources at the disposal of someone."[20] To say that, however, invites us to consider how love functions in the search for a universal humanity.

Here even Marney & [Pelikan] would agree.

For those from a Christian background, Marney suggests (exegeting I Cor. 13) that love is a way of "Christing it" in the world: a way of relating and caring in a Christ-like manner. It is based on an ontological conviction as to who God is; as such it includes faith and

---

[17]*Op. cit.,* p. 8.

[18]"The Language of Revelation," p. 5.

[19]*Ibid.,* p. 7.

[20]*Ibid.,* p. 9.

hope. It moves through and beyond the personal to seek a healing of the body politic; hence it is concerned (as Tillich saw) with power and justice. It has roots in community, hence is intertwined with memory, but always expresses itself in the present. *Love is the critical ingredient in the quest for a universal humanity.* It abides through disappointments, separations, and sufferings. It is not an exclusive mode of Christians. (In fact, it is often strangely missing from those communities which purport most loudly to be Christian!) But it must be the lodestar orienting any community which seeks to move beyond racial, national and social divisions.

Two other traditional theological terms—"death" and "resurrection"—were important for Marney as he pressed the implications of universal humanism. The two terms have to be seen together. In his earlier years, Marney understood death as the final event of the finite and tragic human experience. In this last decade, however, he was moved by the Pauline affirmation that *humanity makes its own death.* Our true destiny, he came to believe, is to transcend death. In despair about death, we fail to discern the plan of God for the whole human species. There is more to the human mystery than biology; here Marney came to identify strongly with Teilhard de Chardin and Polanyi, both of whom testified to a cosmic process which is at work bringing humanity to "an unthinkable consummation."

On the question of "resurrection," we can discern a radical change in Marney from his earlier days. Was it through his own brushes with death through his illness? Was it the process of aging, which itself brings different perspectives and priorities? Or was it a new theological insight, growing out of his exegesis of Paul? These are not mutually exclusive, of course, but the end result is clear: Marney affirms the Pauline vision that God cares for us beyond the grave. He knew that this a mystery, and, as he often did, he resorted to a musical metaphor: the bass solo in Part III of Handel's *Messiah*, which proclaims "We shall be changed!"[21] What this means specifically for a new humanity is that it can live by hope. We need not trust in the perfectibility of human nature, or in the redemption of political structures, or even in the eradication of all diseases; we rather trust in God's ultimate purposes. We know that we live in a *not yet* time of history, but Marney, recalling Handel's indication of a trumpet solo for the triumphant future, felt

---

[21]*The Coming Faith,* pp. 103-05.

(As he neared death, Marney changed as did Lee Atwater! Of given more time, his view of Jesus may also have changed.)

that the "new breed" of person could live confidently and expectantly:

> We live a hope for the permanent. We live expectantly. We live in assurance that the changing changes of the final change do participate in meaning, permanence and fullfillment. And not for us only but for a fantastic company. It—the trumpet Word—is for "all who have the leading of God's Spirit," all who can hear the trumpet—a very special trumpet. It is for all the *ecclesia of God*, composed of all those among whom God has left a witness.[22]

We noted in Chapter III that during his years as a pastor, Marney was most vivid in describing the quandaries of the human situation, and content in his Christology to focus on the Cross as an event which evokes commitment. It is surprising to note that as his theological vision shifted to a more pronounced universal humanism, he simultaneously came to affirm confidently the Christian resurrection proclamation. He wanted no more quibbling, no more reservations, no more disdain for or academic arguments about the nature of the resurrection:

> I am sick of slick presentations that evade the issue. They keep saying, whether resurrection is so or not, we have this, and this, and this, and moral incentive as an effect of whatever resurrection was or was not, is or is not. Piffle! I want it all! Let us trust our future as well as our origins. Let us buy the whole package.
>
> I believe in the Resurrection of the dead! I believe in the Resurrection from among the bodily dead![23]

"We have let our myths too soon!"

We cannot leave this discussion of "The New Humanism and Old Theological Categories" without noting some of the subtleties involved. It is clear that in his last decade Marney wanted to break out of parochial, restrictive senses of Christianity to affirm a broader human fellowship, but at the same time he found meaning in traditional Christian terminology. Marney often acknowledged that we come back to the old symbols because we cannot improve upon them; this seems to be behind his insight into the Pauline "death" and "resurrection" motifs. The terms "incarnation," "revelation," and "love" lent themselves well to Marney's broader vision because they

---

[22]*Ibid.*, p. 112.

[23]*Ibid.*, p. 134.

enabled him to tie the new to the old. This utilization of traditional terms undoubtedly enabled Marney to communicate with Christian audiences, but they also slightly obscure the creative aspects of his theology.

It seems fair to conclude, however, that Marney's brand of humanism was a distinctly religious—and specifically Christian—humanism. It is not precise to say that his new vision had to do only with man; in fact, it had a lot to say about God. It is based on convictions about God's love, God's disclosures in life and history, and God's ultimate purposes. Marney believed that we have access to divine resources, experienced as grace. That conviction kept him rooted in the Christian tradition. It put him in company with such theological interpreters as Ronald Gregor Smith, Roger Shinn, James Luther Adams, and John A.T. Robinson, all of whom were addressing different audiences with similar convictions about Christian humanism. One way of describing the shift in Marney's theological orientation would be to say that in his last decade he took natural theology more seriously than he had before. He was inclined to see the plan of God in and through the biological processes, the rhythms of history, the plurality of religions, and the diversity of cultures. His consistent theme—developed in his own, metaphorical way—was that the deepest understanding of the Judeo-Christian heritage points us outwards toward a religious understanding of the whole world. On one point, however, Marney sounded the same note he had expressed in two earlier decades: we do not hear this deeper understanding proclaimed very often. Most of our churches turn us inwards and not outwards. Our land is still beset by the problem of a superficial Christanity.

The Church and the New Humanism

Marney, never enamored with the institutional church, nevertheless could not escape it. Most of his audiences, after all, were ministers, Church leaders, lay people involved with the Church, or students who were being shaped by it. In the writings and lectures of his last decade, Marney showed a dialectical involvement with the Church. Often he despaired of it, mocking its superficiality, resistance to change, and cultural enslavement; his criticisms were so mordant at times as to imply that any Christian of intelligence or integrity would leave the Church like a sinking ship. At other times, however, he indicated that the great task was to renew the Church, and had definite ideas as to how this might be done. He often quoted Gustav Weigel's wry observation: "In every age, the institutions of religion are dying—but they never do."[24] Realistically we appear to be stuck with our denominational structures; some may not be worth saving, but until they die, whatever can be done to make them more humane ought to be done. Marney is not consistent on this point, however; his vacillation may reflect his different audiences as well as his shifting moods of optimism or pessimism.

We noted in Chapter II that Marney was sharply critical of conventional Church life during his Austin and Charlotte pastorates. He became even more critical during his Interpreter's House years. Some of his friends (particularly those still in the pastorate) resented his critiques, feeling themselves maligned, and believed that Marney often overlooked the ambiguities which they faced in the professional ministry. Some felt that Marney too quickly forgot the nurturing role of pastoral care in local congregations. A few acquaintances of Marney's took the position that once a man leaves the parish ministry, he forfeits his right to criticize the work of other ministers. At any rate, let us consider initially some of Marney's critical observations. In 1970 he wrote:

> The churches, by and large, are closed communions, ghettos, refuges of sick and miserable people. They cling for some kind of mutual confirmation but reproduce in their own bodies every crime and beastly capacity. On the large scale, we are essentially not different from those who are outside. This is the crisis of modern Christianity, and it is a dreadful crisis.[25]

A dominant characteristic of many main-line churches, Marney felt, was the loss of a *raison d'etre*. For those who gather in these churches, "(A)ll of life's deep meanings are threatened by a dreadful pointlessness."[26] People are blocked, not helped, in their quest for personhood, and they choke on mundane, routine rituals. Too frequently the Church has been obsessed by respectability, when in fact "the more respectable you become the more moldly you get, just

---

[24]"Beyond the Denominations," Lecture II of the Dickson Lectures; *op. cit.,* pp. 44-5.

[25]*The Coming Faith,* p. 158.

[26]"The Point of Meeting," a mimeographed lecture delivered at Chautauqua, New York, in July, 1973; p. 3.

like good cheese."[27] The basic function of the church should be to produce a "Pilgrim People"—a group which can see through the myths, institutions, and ideologies of our time, and which can in its life, work, and worship bring us to a "competent manhood."

A church with that vision gets its priorities straight. It knows that all denominational labels are adjectives. The noun, said Marney, is "Man"—Humanity.[28] Any term less encompassing is too limited. Marney felt this point so strongly that at the beginning of his 1974 Dickson Lectures, he announced that it was the last time he wished to be heard as a Baptist.

Obviously such an orientation takes one beyond denominations and even beyond the ecumenical movement as we have known it within Christendom. Authentic life pushes toward synthesis and a new creation, judging obsolete our old forms and structures. The great temptation for all religion, Marney once observed, is the Romantic one: to live in a world already dead.[29] The basic ontological reality, however, is *change*. It is also necessary for life and growth:

> To keep things as they were requires the death of inquiry, the suffocation of intelligence, the emasculation of reason, rigidity in all institutions, and the burial of freedom.[30]

(Here Marney shows his debt to Teilhard and Whitehead.)

The future, whatever else, will bring new associations of people—new "forms of meeting," as Marney liked to say, and a clarification of the real agenda of the Church: the destiny of human beings. Anything less ultimate, e.g., economics, politics, nationalism, sex, race, family mores, religious institutions, are *problems* but not fundamental issues. Confusion on this point has been one of the tragedies of the contemporary scene; in religion, we have replaced the noun, "Man," with strings of adjectives which are not worth our loyalty; in education, we have succumbed to pressures for specialization so fracturing our knowledge that to speak with a wise voice becomes impossible; in technology we have let commercial interests so distort our values that we cooperate in despoiling the earth and laying the seeds for the destruction of humanity. Sadly, the churches have been

---

[27]"Hail and Farewell," *op. cit.,* p. 37.

[28]*Ibid.,* p. 35.

[29]*Ibid.,* p. 48.

[30]*Ibid.,* p. 49.

so implicated in this distortion of values and priorities that they have lost the moral imperative. They are, with few exceptions, more a part of the problem than of the answer.

Can redemption come from within the churches? Marney became dubious about this, and frequently said in his later years that religious renewal would come through small groups working outside denominational structures. Sometimes he suggested that "community," not Church, is the critical category, and that renewal (i.e., self-correction, self-reorientation) could take place only "among friends who care about Christ," and not within the institutional church. Our real Church, in fact, is found in "whatever little group in Christ you are beginning to be able to trust."[31] In a particularly pessimistic mood he once concluded that the denominations are "dead." They are no longer salt.

> They are mere bookkeeping devices to protect the vested interests. . . Let the denominations go — and join the revolt that really matters.[32]

Consistent with this notion that our nurturing communities may well be outside the formal structures of the Church, Marney continued to hammer (as he did at Myers Park) on the concept of vocation. He stressed the possibilities for redemptive work within the callings of different occupations. He praised the dedication of a few scientists he had known (such as a scientist at Cornell who spent his lifetime working on diseases of the common potato). He saw hope in family counselors who try to help resolve domestic discord, in diplomats committed to peaceful solutions to volatile political problems, in judges who seek the good rather than the letter of the law, in young people in the peace corps, attorneys who work for other than personal gain, and in creative ecologists, teachers, businessmen, psychiatrists, housewives, and pharmacologists. These are the "new priests," Marney claimed, and could so function because the vision of universal humanism breaks down the old barriers of sacred and secular.[33]

But let us look now at the other side of the coin. If one is bound to the Church as institution, or entrusted with leadership within it, are there any options for renewal? When Marney addressed groups of

---

[31] *Priests to Each Other*, p. 75.

[32] *Ibid.*, p. 117.

[33] *Ibid.*, pp. 58-60.

Church leaders, he occasionally showed modest optimism. Marney's files yielded two sets of lectures which are instructive at this point: one series on how the Church's life is related to the rhythms of liturgy, delivered at Chautauqua, New York, in July of 1973; and another set on "The Church in the Modern World" delivered at an Evangelism Seminar for Methodist ministers at the Interpreter's House in February, 1975. Various sermons and lectures given at the Interpreter's House likewise suggest that Marney saw some possibilities for renewal (if not total redemption!) of the churches. An idea frequently stressed was that churches might take the dynamics of small groups more seriously. He was moved by the classic phrase which opens Ruel Howe's volume *The Miracle of Dialogue*: "Every man you meet is a potential adversary," and stressed that personal wholeness requires a setting that enables people to remove their debilitating masks. We are all wanting:

> How great our needs, how dependent the richest of us, how
> hungry the most obese of us, how frustrated the most secure
> of us, how deep your cleavage, how broad your ambitions,
> how empty your power because how short your time. How
> presumptuous. . . all our claims, and how real our death.[34]

Churches, with their penchant for bureaucratic organization and increasing size, treat persons as one-dimensional entities. There is no renewal without personal encounter; Marney reminded his listeners that nothing important ever happens to people in casual meetings or services. Only when churches can help people discover the dimension of depth does grace become a possibility.

What does it mean to discover this "dimension of depth"? It means to take guilt seriously, hence to recognize our common vulnerability and our mutual needs. Marney's person-centered theology meant for him that life in the Church must be earnest to be redemptive. His language is closely related to that of Tillich and John A.T. Robinson. Grace comes when we can admit our despair, our failures, our violation of those whom we love, our perpetuation of habits of which we are not proud. It comes to us in communities and relationships when we first learn that we can be accepted in spite of what we are. It comes when we give and receive acts of kindness. It comes when we see other people who have been made whole. It is present in all acts of mercy. When persons can "bless their own origins," acknowledge and

---

[34]"Behind the Mask," N. D., mimeographed sermon, p. 2.

claim their roots, for better or worse, and admit the contradictions of life, then they can help to make grace. Marney felt that this insight was captured profoundly in the title of Henri Nouwen's *The Wounded Healer.* "In the army of the Lord," Marney liked to say, "all are wounded."[35]

Any healing community, then, will be a community of acceptance and forgiveness. How rare that is among Protestant churches, wedded to hypocritical standards of propriety, custom, and morality! What a revolution awaits any community that dares to proclaim and live out forgiveness. Every pastor knows the differences between the public faces and the private lives of his parishioners, as well as the webs of deceit which so often shape the mentality of religious communities. Marney (showing an indebtedness to Karl Menninger) knew that many people are filled with self-hatred; that lives are lived out in patterns of self-destruction; and that many of our deepest emotional wounds are self-inflicted. "Whatever forgiveness may mean it will have to begin here where we are maiming ourselves."[36] That is why the first step to wholeness is to learn to love *ourselves*—and any Church which would be a channel of grace must understand that.

Can churches as we know them help people to love themselves? This does not mean, of course, to reinforce narcissism or middle class smugness. It means to drive deep into the contradictions of life and to face what we instinctively want to avoid: the marks of finitude, the limitations of knowledge, our uncertain life spans, the imperfection of everything human. Only when we admit and face our errors of judgment, our years of pursuing the wrong goals, and the reality of unredemptive suffering will we be able to affirm life beyond the contradictions. That is finally what self-love (or self-acceptance) means. It has one inescapable corollary: that we must stop trying to use the Eternal as a crutch to escape our human limitations. Life has to be lived out courageously, fully aware of its paradoxes, before we can authentically pray the Kyrie Eleison: "Lord have mercy."[37]

Another possible method of renewal is for the Church to serve as a *conscience* for the broader community. In this role it "listens" for the

[35]"Healers or Curers," (mimeographed), the Sanger Lecture at the Medical College of Virginia, 1976, pp. 4-6.

[36]"Behind the Mask," *op. cit.,* p. 6.

[37]Marney develops this theme in his lecture "Kyrie Eleison," delivered at Chautauqua, New York, in July, 1973; pp. 1-3.

weeping of society: for the sighs of the disinherited, for the pleas of those who come to join its ranks. It knows that it is only a channel for a Kingdom that is to come, and it resists the temptation to make itself ultimate. For renewal in this sense, more meaningful *worship* is necessary. Worship is at its best when it leads us through the rhythms of confessing, hearing, forgiveness, and renewal. (Whatever ambiguities or ironies Marney saw in the institutional church, he always took worship seriously.) Worship—well planned and responsively entered into—can be a means of grace, and those entrusted with its leadership would do well to take this task more seriously.

Churches which embrace the vision of Christian humanism must also come to grips with the problem of adult education. No church can be a vital community if it is made up of those who can never have a new religious thought after age sixteen: those for whom "the death of inquiry has come, and the search is over."[38] Marney returned to this theme again and again. Churches have to *grow* in the process of becoming a Pilgrim people. All growth, in turn, comes out of new experience, both inside and outside the Church; and if the Church is to present a mature gospel to maturing men and women, it has to have an educational program that is theologically sound and personally relevant. An educational system clarifies the implications of stewardship, evangelism, and service; without better education the Church is doomed to perpetual mediocrity, or worse — to the pursuit of false gods.

The basic point I have attempted to clarify in this section is that Marney had a lover's quarrel with the Church as an institution: he could not unequivocally embrace it, nor could he escape it. While criticizing the denominations, he was still funded by them as he developed the Interpreter's House. But whether Christian humanism will flourish outside the churches or within them, Marney insisted that "God will not have Christianity as it is!"[39] Given that, it is not surprising that Marney also seriously addressed the dilemmas of ordained ministers.

---

[38]"Strong Meat for a Full Age," one of a series of lectures Marney gave on "The Church in the Modern World," at the Interpreter's House, January 20 - February 24, 1975. The lecture is mimeographed; cf. p. 9.

[39]*The Coming Faith*, p. 149.

The Ministry and the New Humanism

Although Marney explored this theme in numerous lectures both at the Interpreter's House and around the country, his major written work on this topic was his volume *Priests to Each Other* (1974), cited already several times in this study. At several points this book yokes concerns for the ministry with concerns about the Church; it also raises specific questions about the role and function of the professional clergy. "What if a kept clergy is always a harlotry?.," he asked for openers.[40] He noted how deprecatingly ordained clergy tend to speak of laypeople, and was critical of clerical assumptions that elevate the clergy over laypeople. His evaluation of the clergy, even as he empathized with and healed their bruises at the Interpreter's House, was that as a group they are "incompetent and off-balance." He was once quoted as saying "Ninety percent of the clergy we see do not have sufficient sense of integrity or ego maturity to say 'boo' to a church mouse, far less a culture."[41] Marney persistently encouraged clergy to take the laity more seriously:

> The aim of the church is not to enlist its laymen in its services; the aim is to put laymen and theological competents in the service of the world.[42]

Just as Marney showed some ambivalence about the renewability of the Church, so he obviously had ambivalent feelings about the role of professional ministers in the Church's future. Much of *Priests to Each Other* is geared to the creation of a new breed of responsible laypeople, but it also explores the implications of this for those who are ordained. Clergy, too, will need to shed their masks; they will have to find wholeness themselves before they can minister to others. They will have to see through the ministry's "professional deformations" — the ideological cocoon which enables a person to go through a career "hiding behind a swarm of comforting convictions about himself which follow him like fleas on a warm dog."[43] Integrity in the ministry will come only when clergy can be honest enough to explore their motives, their ego needs, their defensiveness, and their uncritical

---

[40]*Priests to Each Other*, p. 8.

[41]Quoted in his citation from the University of Glasgow upon the occasion of his being awarded the D.D. Degree, June 23, 1976. The text comes from Marney's files.

[42]*Priests to Each Other*, pp. 14-15.

[43]"Behind the Masks," p. 2.

acceptance of cultural ideology. There is no easy road for ministers - no short cuts which spare them from the hard journey inward on the way to healing.

In his last years (1975-78) Marney was increasingly involved with the tragedies of the professional ministry. In talks to ministers' conferences, he often referred to ministers as "tragic men," borrowing a line from Benjamin Mays, who once referred to Billy Graham's preaching in the Nixon White House as "the most tragic man in the most tragic house." Marney's description of the typical professional holy man was as follows:

> In America, at least (and if he wants a job or a better job) he is under 39, a graduate of a respectable seminary, and possesses a "personal magnetism." He is something of a civic leader, but knows how to avoid bad publicity. He has no radical social ideas, no *new* preachment, and has a way with young people. He can be fiery without being personal, looks like a man of the world, but emits a faint aura of probable saintliness. He is a good mixer, uses impeccable English, is a fair enough golfer, wears tweeds well, takes one highball, knows the jargon of his trade, and in committee is apt to be modestly authoritarian.[44]

Marney developed a set of metaphors to describe these tragic men: even on our best days (note that he included himself) we know ourselves to be *shaken reeds*, vacillating with each blowing wind; we are *smoking lamps*, sputtering and even smothered by the rages of our culture; we are *earthen vessels*, "absorbing and passing along in our gospels the extracts of our own prejudiced, provincial places;" and we are *untempered mortar*, unable to hold anything or to bind anything among the new structures in the world of thought. Sometime around age fifty ministers become *spent arrows*, exhausted from the futility of struggling against culture, disillusioned with their achievements, but still hoping for some affirmation of how they have invested their time. As a group they command little respect; history seems to have passed them by.

It is both interesting and important, if we are to understand Marney's sense of the professional ministry, to ask *why* he felt ministers to be "tragic men." As a professional group they are neither

---

[44]"A Lost Manhood," unpublished lecture, N.D., I have edited this quotation slightly for clarity.

better nor worse than other comparable groups. The answer to this question is suggested more in Marney's unpublished notes than in his published works. Ministers become tragic men when they are beholden to denominational or congregational structures for their means of existence. Young prophets are usually co-opted into systems and structures which control them; they buy in so deeply that they can no longer speak or act as men of conscience. Men and women who at one time aspired to a prophetic role become house priests because of economic necessities. The professional ministry as we know it is beholden to a culture that follows after other gods than Yahweh. It is in this sense that the "tragic men" live in "tragic houses."

It was this sense of tragedy, I believe, which prompted Marney to probe for new patterns of ministry, both in a revised sense of calling for lay persons, and also in the model of "worker-priests" (or perhaps more accurately, "worker-prophets"). There is a place for those specially trained in theological studies, to be sure, but their integrity as religious leaders will be far less compromised if they have other means of financial support. Much of Marney's work at the Interpreter's House dealt with those who had no economic alternatives for themselves or their families. The ambiguities of denominational politics, the aspirations for professional "success," and the economic reality of governing boards of local churches all tremendously complicate ministerial identity and integrity. Marney knew that; he had been there himself.

Marney was wise enough to know, however, that most ministers are unable to extricate themselves from the webs which both sustain and entrap them. His exhortations were therefore tempered by his sense of what is possible in a less than ideal situation. On numerous occasions, he stressed two modes of growth and redirection for these "tragic men." Renewal can come through *intellectual reorientation*, moving away from the academic and dogmatic categories of traditional theology and toward a theology of persons. The time is past due for such a theological shift to take place in the seminaries. It would mean utilizing new sources for theological education: such thinkers as Paul Tournier, Denis de Rougemont, Karl Menninger, Sigmund Freud, Ruel Howe, and Abraham Maslow. If ministers first learn to be *men*, then they can eventually become men *of God*. That new awareness will minimally clarify for ministers the distorted priorities of cultural Christianity and can sharpen what the real purpose of ministry is all about.

Secondly, ministers must develop the capacity to *hear*. "My seminary taught me a lot about speaking," Marney once observed, "but they didn't teach me a thing about listening."[45] In our desire to explicate God (and Marney felt increasingly in his last years that all ministers say more than they know), we have been oblivious to the needful and crippled persons who make up our flocks. Such people do not need prophetic denunciation; they need faith, hope, and unconditional love. Here again we note how Marney's humanistic orientation suggests alternate models of ministry. He often suggested that ministers would be better channels of grace if they preached less and listened more, and expressed doubts about the cumulative value of his own years of preaching. In a poignant recollection Marney once acknowledged that in the course of his own parish days he knew that people often needed counseling more than preaching:

> On the Sundays my ego could stand it, I looked out the window of the sanctuary study to watch the people going home after Church School and before Morning Worship. But always my eye fell too on another parade: the people dragging or pushing their burdens into the Sanctuary, where across the French Walnut pew tops I would have to face them presently. To some, to many of them I wanted to call out, "Don't go in there! Let's talk — 'twould be better than this preaching at *all* of us."[46]

Marney experienced for himself the deeper reaches of a listening ministry at the Interpreter's House, and often used illustrations from his work there to illumine his own path of growth.

Marney was convinced that there is a solid theological basis for this re-orientation of ministry. Ultimately it is a correlative of the Incarnation: God's hallowing of human life. The divine entered the realm of the human and blessed it. Persons count, and grace is present to enable us to be more than we have been. Ministers committed to Christian humanism know that more than logical and technological structures frame our thoughts and our societies. The reality of grace gives integrity to the ministry.

Such were Marney's views in his more optimistic moments, once he acknowledged that denominations, like other human institutions,

---

[45]"Fundaments of Competent Ministry", a mimeographed lecture, N.D., p. 2.

[46]"A Proper Forgiveness," a lecture at Chatauqua, New York, in July, 1973, p. 4.

were not going to fade away. It sometimes appears that his thoughts about renewal for ordained clergy were attempts to make the most out a bad situation. The malignancy which infects both the denominations and the ministry is widespread and nothing short of radical surgery will suffice. I think it is clear that if Marney were empowered to redraw the map of Christendom, he would do it without denominational lines, and probably without the professional ministry as we know it.

The Reappraisal of Religious Language

In Chapter II I quoted one of Marney's friends who called him "a mountaineer with the soul of a poet." Anyone who ever heard Marney speak understood that description, but it is apt to be misleading for theological analysis. As a preacher Marney turned phrases, spoke metaphorically, told stories, etched visions, and captured imaginations. As a theologian as well, he knew that language was power. As a medium it shaped the substance of faith and values. He came to see that much of the dilemma of contemporary Christendom was related to the misuse of language. Culture changes faster than our vocabularies, and of all modes of discourse, religious language is the last to change. In a typical Protestant congregation (whose language is "colonial, generally Confederate, white, provincial, unilateral, even pre-Copernican"[47]), anyone who talks about religion has to speak in language four hundred years out of date or he won't be heard. One who would speak the truth must deal with the nuances of language. Marney searched for language that transcended any given view of the universe; only such words "can be expected to have carry-over value to that new age which is always born along with a new world-view."[48] Underlying the search for new language, however, is one constant Reality: the God known as a loving Father.

Some words out of the Christian tradition (English translations, to be sure) remain with us — words like "love-hate, believe-obey, hope, faith, good, heart, give, man, hand, household, remember, expect, have, do, be, Father." They are short, simple, suggestive, authentic. Many of our most-repeated expressions, however, are basically confusing and no longer relevant: "The blood of the Lamb," "Have you met the Lord?", "A spiritual person," "Do the Lord's bidding," "Going to heaven." Terms such as these are either trite or based on an

---

[47]"The Language of Faith," N.D., a mimeographed lecture; p. 3.

[48]*Ibid.,* p. 4.

outmoded worldview. They are symptomatic of a static, antiquated mentality and of a religious ennui. Their use plagues all denominations but is especially bad in evangelical Protestantism. Their emotional roots cause them to linger in minds which in most other ways are informed and responsible. Marney insisted that there will be no religious breakthroughs, no new humanity, until we can recover the power of *primal* words: words that speak of our relationship to God, to neighbor, and to our own depths.

Marney called these primal words "relational language." He contrasted such language with its antithesis, "functional" language, which speaks of impersonal structures, static entities, legalisms, amd statistics. Relational verbs are verbs that go between personal pronouns; relational language occurs anywhere an I and a Thou are related.[49] The language of relation can therefore be called the language of being: it is "clear, direct, open, honest and simple." It uses no phony titles or phony talk of love, but it is nevertheless emotional. It speaks of meetings, encounters, transformations. It understands communities, obligations, loyalties, symbolism, and ambiguity. It interprets change in dynamic categories. It is, above all, a *process* language. In this sense it is faithful to biblical language, which is "a language of beginning, continuing, toward a promised end not yet in view."[50] Much of the bewilderment and disappointment of ministers is related to the fact that they are trying to speak in relational language while conventional pew sitters are thinking in functional language. To help people move from one mode of discourse to the other is a difficult and time-consuming task, but it is essential for meaningful nurture and Christian education.

Marney announced in his Dickson Lectures of 1974 that he was also dropping from his religious vocabulary a whole range of words which have become cliches: "renewal, orthodox, sound (as in when a person is said to be theologically "sound"), sanctification, edification (we see too little of these phenomena to understand what they mean anymore), indoctrinate, organize and joint effort." There was a touch of humor in Marney's remarks, but it was humor with an edge. He had heard these words too many times from denominational drum-beaters or from advance men for various causes. Marney wanted his hearers to become sophisticated enough to see through the hyperbolic use of these old terms.

---

[49]*Ibid.*, p. 9.

[50]*Ibid.*, p. 15.

Sensitivity to the structure of language can also help us be more precise in approaching the mystery of God and the nature of faith. Too often we have spoken of God in the nominative case. We should rather learn to speak of God in the dative case—as One "to whom something is given, told or shown." Faith, so often depicted in the passive voice, needs to be recast in the active voice, for it is "the demand for obedience to light I already have."[51] Faith is the way we live out our values, visions, and loyalties; it is, at its best, the basis of an active way of being, not just a passive way of thinking. In our earlier discussion on the Church we noted how Marney drew the distinction between adjectives ("Baptist, Christian") and the basic noun they modify ("Humanity"). The point here is to illustrate how Marney utilized grammatical categories to clarify the ontological errors in contemporary religious thinking.[52]

It should be acknowledged, however, that Marney showed little familiarity with recent linguistic analysis which sees grammatical categories as inextricably related to the world view of the people who use the language. That we *have* an active and passive voice says something about our perception of reality and how we are in the world. In a culture, for example, whose language had no passive voice, ontological reflection would take place in a wholly other framework.

It is also worth noting at this point that Marney's interests in religious language have more in common with the theologians of Personal Being whom we described in Chapter III (Ortega, Buber, Unamuno, Berdyaev, and MacMurray) than they have with the tradition of religious language analysis spawned by the British school of linguistic philosophy. Marney never seriously entered the debates over the verification of God-claims or the epistemology of empiricism. Marney simply assumed what most theologians of religious language (e.g., Ian Ramsey, Fred Ferre, John Macquarrie) sought to prove, namely, that behind our world is a personal God who cares for us and whom we can trust. I do not think it necessarily follows that Marney would denigrate the significance of those who probed the nature of religious language in a more empirical, critical manner. For Marney and his agenda, however, such endeavors are a part of academic, and not personal or pastoral, theology.

---

[51] *Priests to Each Other,* p. 114.

[52] Although the lectures of Marney's were in some instances revised for publication, his original lecture titles were "The Language of Faith," "The Language of Revelation," and "The Language of Conversion and Revolution."

Transitions in Ethics

The reorientation to a broader humanism had important consequences for Marney as an ethicist. We noted in Chapter III that Marney was not an ethicist in any technical, academic sense of that term; but in various lectures and sermons during this last decade of his life, he developed a number of themes about a new life style. These evolving principles do not reject the ethical insights which we noted in Chapter III as much as they go beyond them, mirroring some of the shifts in Marney's own life as well as the new issues of a changing theological climate. Let us now consider these new ethical emphases in detail. Four themes predominate in his writings, sermons, and lectures.

a. *Our Essence is in our Being.* In an early lecture from the Interpreter's House entitled "To Have, To Do and To Be" (subsequently revised and published as "The Grammar of Faith" in *Priests to Each Other)*, Marney contrasted the notion that Christianity is something that one *has* or *does* with the idea that Christianity is something that a person *is*. If we think of religion (any religion!) as something we have—a possession of sorts—we are always setting ourselves up for disappointments. With that mentality, we are unable to deal with change, new knowledge, new categories, and can only utilize static, functional language. If we conceive of religion as something we "do," we get caught up in a frenzy of activities that add to the harassment of our lives but give us no redemption: we "fix flowers, wait tables, plan a program, do a good, raise a budget, buy a preacher, hire a specialist, donate stock."[53] Of course there is a human propensity to identify ourselves by what we *have* (cars, boats, clothes, stock, houses) and *do* (our professions, vocations, achievements, vita sheets), but authentic Christianity is a matter of *being*:

> It means a willingness to be as one is without any direct object. He is as he is, warts and all. To be is to be, even without arms and legs; one could almost say without mind. To be is to be whether one is sick or well, crippled, dumb, blind or rich. To be is to be without defense, possession, excuse, power, energy or will. It is never to be *what* . . . Being is just being.[54]

---

[53]See "The Language of Faith," p. 8.

[54]*Priests to Each Other,* p. 45.

Marney illustrated this point with a story from his parish ministry days. He spoke of a female teenage paraplegic, without hands or legs, a strong voice, or mobility, who was asked by an insensitive social worker if she wouldn't as soon be done with it all. The girl cheerfully replied, "I wouldn't have missed being for anything."

All genuine Christianity, then, rests on this awareness of the Christian essence: we have worth not because of what we have or what we do, but because all life, even our individual one, is hallowed, affirmed, grasped by God. This realization can open us outwards; it offers the possibility of depthful relationships which we can accept; it imbues us with confidence and hope.

Even though Marney could speak theoretically about the centrality of being, through most of his life his intense schedule seemed to testify to an ethic of action. For many years Marney *was* an advocate of people acting to ameliorate human hurt. If pressed he would always say that the deeds are by-products of a new sense of being, but to bear a witness (i.e., be a part of purposive endeavors) was an important Christian attribute. During the years when his health failed and he spent time quietly in convalescence, Marney realized the value of withdrawal and renewal. "It is all right to be who you are," he often said. Undoubtedly the mellowing of his own years was a factor in this transition, but Marney in his sixth decade was more confident than he was in his third decade of God's hallowing our being.

b. *An Ethic of Parsimony.* By the mid-1970's Marney realized, as did most other responsible Christian leaders, that the limits of the world's resources required a reappraisal of western life styles. This is not just a matter of facing the inevitable. It is also a recognition that Creation has limits; it is limited by *systems* (neural, blood, bone, cellular) *processes* (phylo-genetic, bio-chemical, photo-synthetic), and by *spheres* (biosphere, nousphere, hemisphere). For Marney this called for an "ethic of parsimony": learning how to live with the least that will suffice, thus bringing our lives into a closer harmony with the created order.

For a consumer society which has lived as though creation had no limits, this requires a radical reassessment of priorities. It calls for more than frugality or penury (a sort of spiritual distortion); it seeks a cogent and realistic assessment of what is necessary to meet our daily needs. Consistent with this is a fresh concern for being good stewards of nature's resources. I have found no sources to indicate that Marney ever applied this principle to an analysis of energy sources, food supplies, or environmental issues, but it is clear that Marney discerned and responded to the signs of the times with this theme of parsimony. It is regrettable that Marney did not live to develop this insight more specifically, but even so it is consistent with Marney's approach to ethics which we noted in Chapter III: He tended to be stronger on principles than on applying those to concrete problems.[55]

c.   *An Ethic of Responsibility.* Responsibility is the mode of life lived by covenants. We are bound to God for the well-being of nature, and bound to care for those with whom we covenant in life: spouses, children, parents, friends, colleagues, our communities, and, ultimately, the human family. No one lives in complete self-sufficiency or acts without consequences. Given the importance of this theme in modern ethics through the work of H. Richard Niebuhr, James Gustafson, and others, it is surprising that Marney was so late in emphasizing it. Again Marney did not develop it in detail, but I believe we can get insights into his intention if we consider two of his best-known sermons of this decade, "In the Meantime"(based on Jeremiah 29:4-13) and "When Wisdom Flirts with Madness" (an exposition of Ishmael's famous line in *Moby Dick*: "There is wisdom that is love but there is a woe that is madness.").

The sermon "In the Meantime" stresses that most of life is lived waiting for something. Conditions are never just right. We live in expectation of something that is ahead. What does this mean for living responsibly?

> How can I live when my heart is somewhere else? How can I make it when my dreams have no prospect of coming true? How can I work when my hope is so distant from its consummation? How can I grow in this captivity of mine? How can I endure the silence when I long for strident sound and the singing voices? How can I see in this darkness when my eyes were made for light?[56]

The clue for redeeming the "meantimes" of life is in taking hold where we are—doing the things that are required. Purposive life does not wallow in the thought of what might have been, but builds on what

---

[55]See his sermon preached at Duke in 1978, "A Christian Life Style," *op. cit.*, pp. 1-4.

[56]"In the Meantime," a mimeographed sermon, N.D., p. 2. Marney's files revealed that he had received more requests for copies of this sermon than for any other he had preached.

is needed and possible where we are. The mundane, ordinary responsibilities of home and family life; the work which needs to be done; the establishment of roots: without such activities we lose hope. God's healing occurs as we faithfully do the prosaic in the present time. Marney's homiletical message is consistent with what he developed in more formal perspectives on ethics: responsibility means taking hold *now*, not making excuses, not rationalizing our failures, not requiring others to carry our burdens, not yielding to defeat or despair. It means to honor our covenants, to care for what has been entrusted to us, and to be confident that God's grace can be known wherever we are.

The sermon "When Wisdom Flirts with Madness" comes at the issue of responsible life from another angle. The mature person perceives the world's madness: wars, the arms race, discrimination, fanaticism, indifference to suffering, hypocrisy. But these things do not negate the realities of growth, grace, kindness, love, and healing. The wisdom that sees through the rigidity of structures and the idolatries of mass movements becomes madness when it turns to cynicism and a loss of hope for the human future. The responsible person does not let the ubiquity of madness keep him from finding and identifying with the small communities which are agents of reconciliation. Neither do we let our failure to love perfectly keep us from loving as best we can. To be responsible amid the world's capriciousness means to face all that makes us shamed and uncomfortable, and to continue to press for the love that lies beneath the woe.

From the standpoint of ethics, Marney did not deal as much as we might like with the troublesome problem of conflicting responsibilities, but he placed strong emphasis on conscience, the priority of our covenants, and the need for a purposive, steady life pilgrimage which is not thrown off track by personal defeats or the persuasiveness of evil. He seemed confident that our identity in Jesus Christ, which transcends the ordinary labels we use to describe ourselves (families, schools, political parties, race, sex), enables us to care for each other. It impels us to be more than we ordinarily are.

d. *The Common Good.* It is clear that during most of his career Marney directed ethical concerns toward the individual person struggling to make sense of life. He sought to go beyond that in his later years. On numerous occasions, sometimes speaking to Church audiences and sometimes to political or civic assemblies, he stressed the importance of a corporate vision of "The Common Good." In his colorful way, Marney acknowledged that such a vision would not be easily embraced:

> That old saw! That subterfuge of politicians! That old banner of a worn-out Burkeian aristocracy! The chimera Communism fostered and festered over the heads and guts of a billion, four hundred million people! *A Common Good!* Whom do you kid, friend? That old dead American dream? That utopian fraud? It's as dead as freshman courses in ethics; as moribund as legal morality.[57]

Undismayed, and knowing that the concept is mythic, Marney went on to spell out what he meant by this notion. He drew heavily on the philosophical thought of his old friend Arthur Murphy, former Chairman of the Department of Philosophy at the University of Texas. During the McCarthy era, when Murphy was President of the American Philosophical Society, he gave his presidential address at Toronto on the theme of "The Common Good." There can never be a common good, argued Murphy, as long as each person or segment of society pursues its own interest, or if all are subjected to the same mass pressures. A common good, by contrast, is "the interest that can justify itself as *public* on the terms of equity that apply to all. This distinguishes the ethical agreement that separates a community from a manipulative crowd."[58]

Marney sensed in this concept a vision which could be utilized theologically. It was the next step for that community of people who were outgrowing parochial boundaries and self-interests. A vision of a common good would depend upon a deliberate redirection of individual wills. Without such cohesive elements binding together the diverse factions of society, community is not possible. In short:

> Community in search of a Common Good for all is characterized by processes of rationally self-controlled behavior, professedly common purposes faithfully served, with pledges kept and hoped-for goods achieved in action together.[59]

---

[57]"Our Present Higher Good," a sermon preached at Duke and at Harvard in 1973; mimeographed, p. 6.

[58]"The Common Good," an address delivered at Austin, Texas, on January 6, 1974, to the joint assembly of the Texas Constitutional Convention and the Texas Council of Churches; mimeographed, p. 4.

[59]"Our Present Higher Good," p. 8.

The pursuit of The Common Good means that we have to work with whatever moral understanding we have, with people of diverse backgrounds, within ambiguous and compromising social structures, doing, as Murphy said, "the best we can, in the service of the best we know." This, Marney was convinced, was the deepest ethical impulse of a universal humanism. It brings us within God's redemptive purposes for all of humanity. It is the ethical correlate to the vision of Teilhard, the biological conclusions of Loren Eiseley, the plea of Pope John XXIII in *Pacem in Terris*, and the call to commitment of Michael Polanyi.

Several comments are in order about Marney's vision of the Common Good. On the one hand, it appears to be a modern adaptation of the great biblical symbol of the "Kingdom of God." Marney admitted that "it is the great, unrealized, forever elusive, utterly attractive chimera and dream, common desire and longest hope of mankind. It is what all Christendom would have been about if Christendom had ever been Christian. . . "[60] It has affinities with William Temple's depiction of a Christian Commonwealth, Harnack's conclusion that the real essence of Christianity is the message of "the Fatherhood of God and Brotherhood of Man," and Rauschenbusch's Theology of the Kingdom.

On the other hand, Marney obviously saw in this symbol a way of appealing to those whose roots and value systems are not in the Christian tradition. It is a "trans-religious" concept — an appeal to all women and men of good faith. It is not accidental that Marney used this theme when he addressed the 1974 Texas Constitutional Convention, which was made up of people from diverse racial, political, economic, and religious backgrounds. The notion makes an appeal to conscience: we all really do know better — we know what we need to do to have a better earth. Marney thus (again using the indicative) sought to appeal to the higher elements of human nature.

Ethically, this strategy would be classified as a *teleogical* approach and is consistent with Marney's concern to seek the "good" rather than the "right"; to pursue the spirit rather than the letter of the law; and to be responsible to God for all members of the human family. He summed this up in his address to the Convention, as he focused on the pointed issue of oil depletion allowances:

Had I a voice as a member of this Convention, I think I

---

[60]*Ibid.,* p. 6.

might propose a more general Depletion Allowance: in behalf of depleted women in the towns and on ranches; women in the dives and roadside stands and offices and colleges and little houses; a depletion allowance in behalf of frustrated and wasted childhoods among children of all the racial origins and mixes; a generous depletion allowance for all kinds of warped and twisted young and for the very old."[61]

That says in a few words what a commitment to "the Common Good" might mean.

Critically, inasmuch as Marney never tied this goal to a strategy for realizing it, he opens himself to criticisms of naivete and idealism. That such a vision is idealistic there is no doubt, but I think that emphasis in Marney is deliberate. After years of reflecting realistically on the worst facets of human nature, Marney has now turned to ask: what are the best? If, as Abraham Maslow argued in a different context, we establish that the human being is a choosing, deciding, and seeking creature, then do we not eventually have to ask who is the good chooser, and what is worth choosing? Marney's answer to critics who assert that the goal of a Common Good is too vague or naive would be that we all tend to get so enmeshed in smaller problems that we fail to see the big issues.

In summary, we can discern a number of important shifts from his Austin and Charlotte days in Marney's approach to ethics. He moves from a preoccupation with personal realism (Luther, Freud) to a social idealism (the possibility of self-transcendent choices); from the issue of who or what is a Good Person to the search for a Good Society; from an emphasis on *doing* to a stress on *being*; from an interest in vibrant, intelligent, semi-secular "New Breed" people to an ethic of parsimony and responsibility. These transitions influenced not only his writings but also most of his sermons and lectures of this decade.

The Coming of Wisdom: Reflections on Thirty Years in the Ministry

We have interpreted Marney throughout this study as a man on a pilgrimage. We have noted the change in his priorities and perspectives. Integral to his development was the distillation of wisdom: what he came to believe about the claims of faith, human nature, and the ministry itself. This is not the wisdom of books,

---

[61]*Ibid.*, p. 7.

documents, or authorities; it is the wisdom of lived experience. As he got older and was more prone to reminiscing, four observations emerged.

First, Marney saw with increasing clarity that *all theological systems are tentative.* In his 1974 Dickson Lectures, he said:

> There are three things we ought to know by now: 1) All dogma is constructed, all revelation is through human channels; 2) all form is both sustenance and threat; and, 3) all power is mediated authority, all freedom is limited.[62]

The history of the Church, its crises and theological reflection, shows the interaction of cultural, economic, and political forces with the kerygma. No pure form of the Gospel exists; the message always comes to us through cultural filters. All great statements of faith are historically conditioned; for that reason Marney the Free Churchman was always antithetical to creeds and creedalism. Institutions are both necessary and stifling to creativity. Theologians come and go in a passing parade, but issues stubbornly re-emerge under a different guise.[63] Most crucial for the women and men who would act responsibly in this age, however, is the awareness that God's revelation never comes as propositional truth; no thinker is ever a final guide; and no claim of faith can be taken as definitive. Marney agreed with H. Richard Niebuhr's *bon mot*: "We have notions of the Absolute, but we have no absolute notions."

Second, Marney came to understand that *the Gospel falls on deaf ears because people are so encased in their ideological systems that they cannot hear.* In 1974 he wrote:

> I have wasted half my ministry away from home talking my gospel to people who are kept from hearing me by the stereotypes they have made that I cannot fix. And I've spent half my life at home saying again to people what they did not hear me say.[64]

That awareness is what prompted Marney to insist that there is no redemption unless the message "penetrates sooner or later all these treasured feathers of our views of the self." To know that is to know

---

[62]*Op. cit.,* p. 45; see also *Priests to Each Other*, p. 103.

[63]For Marney's description of the "passing parade" of theologians and issues, see *The Recovery of the Person*, pp. 15-17.

[64]*Priests to Each Other*, p. 79.

that any responsible Christian pastor-theologian has to come to grips with ideology. We have alluded to this idea previously as we considered Marney's views on the ministry, but his final sense of this irony went even deeper: people often cannot hear even when they want to. There is an enormous gap between the ministerial *myths* of what a minister is doing and what in fact is happening. That is why the critical factor in what Marney called "Instrumental Theology" is the matter of myth-breaking.[65]

Third, Marney moved from a) *a long preoccupation with Freud and the unconscious*, to b) *an interest in group life and therapy*, to c) *a higher sense of the person and a vision of the Common Good*. His richest description of these transitions is found in his 1973 sermon "Our Present Higher Good." He points out that his discovery of Freud led him to see that traditional theology was not depthful enough in its understanding of the human person. At the same time, his engagement with Buber (and subsequently with humanistic psychologists) helped him to see that grace comes to us through relationships. As we noted, that insight dominated much of his ministry during his last years in Charlotte and his first years at the Interpreter's House. Finally, however, Marney came to see the limitations of that means of redemption:

> I know veterans of twenty "groups" who have fallen off into a kind of escapism; or worse, a sort of invalidism waiting to be rescued; or worse, a fundamental vampirism which feeds on the intestinal content of other members, never revealing the self.[66]

Marney insists that his intellectual pilgrimage was not a *cul de sac* nor a distortion of the Gospel at any particular point. There was (and *is!*) truth in each phase; the insights of each stage have not so much been denied as transcended into something higher. Ultimately he came to feel that as human beings, we have to assume that we can deal with our inwardness; the real task is to seek a purposive life and commit ourselves to a universal humanism.

Fourth, Marney changed his mind considerably as to *what constitutes a good minister*. After thirty years he felt that ministers need to talk less and hear more; they don't need to be book smart but

---

[65]See Marney's lecture, "Fundaments of Competent Ministry," mimeographed, p. 8.

[66]*Loc. cit.*, p. 3.

they need lots of common sense. A good senior minister needs to trust his colleagues and support their special interests in ministry; he need not be a talented administrator, or one who knows about everything that is going on. Much of his success, in fact, is related to having enough common sense to get out of his colleagues' way. Most importantly, however, a minister does not have to be all things to all people:

> I am not God; I do not have to "be a blessing"; I do not have to hear all who "offer" to talk, or make a demand. I can say no to those who threaten me overwhelmingly until we can find a better ground to talk on and I may even send some away empty, for I have been emptied too. A man does not have to lie — and salvation belongs to God.[67]

As a result of his maturing perspectives on the ministry, Marney also changed his mind on who is responsible (not always the preacher!), about what should be done in Christian education programs (more open-ended), and about what makes someone an "expert." He also came to a different understanding of what we can expect from God and what sorts of things we are responsible for ourselves. (Generally, Marney assumed that the earth is our responsibility, and that we will become agents of grace as we set ourselves to the tasks which have to be done.)

Finally, Marney saw that the religious life is *not so much a matter of knowledge as it is of faith.* Through much of his career he was haunted with the realization that we know little about God; "the limits of my knowledge lie closer into shore than I like."[68] He called himself a *docta ignorantia* (a teacher of ignorance), and concluded that before God it is not as important to be *right* as it is to have the nerve to submit to God's claim upon us. The ultimate source of faith will always be a mystery to us. We can neither express nor contain its reality. Yet faith always invites us to commitment; it requires an act of will; it troubles our conscience. Faith varies in intensity and always exists in a dialectic with doubt, but the deep, mysterious claim of God will not let us rest content. Augustine and Richard Niebuhr both influenced Marney on this point, and as he got older he saw that in the life of faith, the heart is more central than the mind.

---

[67] *Priests to Each Other,* p. 113.

[68] *Ibid.,* p. 114.

Summary

Our assessment of Marney's theological development in his last decade has clarified a number of important shifts: he was more optimistic about God's purposes for the created order, and moved to a more distinct teleological orientation both in theology and ethics. He felt confirmed by the work of natural scientists, philosophers, and theologians who spoke of God's design and ultimate purposes in creation. That in turn led him to affirm the concept of resurrection more vigorously than he had before. Even if the reality to which it points is a mystery, surely it can be affirmed joyously and confidently. The roots of this major transition are hard to explicate, but surely his illnesses — which brought him to the brink of death — were as important as his re-discovery of the Apostle Paul. His engagement with Paul's thought, interestingly enough, opened up a new dialogue for him with Karl Barth.

As we noted, Marney in this process became more Christocentric, although he used the concepts of "Christ" and "Incarnation" primarily to emphasize the universality of humanity. All of Marney's listeners and readers know how frequently and convincingly he used those terms; this chapter attempted to clarify what he *meant* by them and how they relate to his basic message of a Christian humanism.

Marney liked to speak of his theological orientation as "relational" (i.e., dialogical, person-centered, direct) or as "instrumental" (i.e., never an end in itself and always in the dative case.) "It knows that God Almighty is nominative case, always subject, but it uses the name haltingly and with a proper stammer."[69] When we keep our talk about our relationship to God in the dative case, we acknowledge that we can speak more confidently and intimately about the Kingdom of God than about its King. This way of describing theological language was rooted in Marney's interests in theological language.

Marney was more aware in his last decade of the extensive power of evil.

> . . . all our legal, penal, educational, religious, governmental and commercial systems are geared to deal with our sinfulness but none really is set up to deal with Evil.[70]

---

[69] "Fundaments of Competent Ministry," p. 4.

[70] "Not To Condemn Us," a sermon preached at Duke on April 17, 1977; mimeographed, p. 4.

Obviously Marney hoped that a vision of The Common Good might be a corrective. Before we can grasp that vision, however, we must have a "mature guilt"—not just a regret for our concupiscense, envy, and greed, but also an awareness of the mass crimes which beset humanity: war, famine, pestilence, and death.

In his own way—and far earlier than the term was developed in its present usage—Marney was a "liberation theologian." He wanted to liberate his hearers and readers from the ideologies which bound them, which kept them from hearing, and which blocked them in their search for full humanization. The great text of Luke 4:18, where Jesus quotes the prophet Isaiah, is often cited by today's Liberation Theologians:

> The Spirit of the Lord is upon me,
> because he has anointed me to preach
> good news to the poor.
> He has sent me to proclaim release to
> the captives
> and recovering of sight to the blind,
> to set at liberty those who are oppressed,
> to proclaim the acceptable year of the Lord. (RSV)

Today's Liberation Theologians are concerned to "release the captives." Marney sought to bring sight to the blind.

CHAPTER V

CONCLUSION: MARNEY IN PERSPECTIVE

One mountaineer said, "Every person is unique." The second mountaineer said, "Yes, but some are more unique than others."

—Thomas A. Langford, "Carlyle Marney," in *Duke Divinity School in Ministry*, August, 1978, p. 4.

The Man and The Message

Many readers of the foregoing chapters may have found the theological analysis interesting but unsatisfying, for they will have different memories or perceptions of Marney. Some will recall him as a fireside story-teller on Texas ranches; some will recall his humorous give-and-take with ministers or laypeople at various assemblies; some adults will remember his teaching them as teenagers in church membership classes; some former students at the Duke Divinity School will remember him as a critical but helpful professor of homiletics. Paducah townspeople will remember that he liked to sing; Austin folk will remember his appeals for the Mexican mission churches and his spontaneous prayers at Wednesday night prayer meetings. Some military chaplains, and many enlisted men, will remember him as a retreat leader and a preacher who made sense in boots and a fatigue jacket in Korea. Some close friends will remember how, armed with a bottle of spirits, he would stay up all night to discuss the Civil War and how he liked to roam around its great battlefields. Participants in seminars at the Interpreter's House will remember his search for integrity, his concern to give them a safe place, and his candor with them. Parishioners at Riverside Church in New York will recall him as a very unusual Southerner, indeed. Adults who were teenagers in Charlotte in the 1960's will remember how he spoke to them upon their high school graduations and urged them to go to college with open hearts and minds.

People wherever he served will recall some of his distinctive characteristics: his life-long tendency to speak to little children by dropping down to their eye level; his ease of conversation with farmers, laborers, and mountaineers ("real people," he called them); how quickly his gruff manner could turn to compassion when he sensed a human problem; his love of horses, apple trees, rabbits, and nature; his dislike of pretense and social veneer. Chautauqua folk of the northeast will remember the style and humor of his platform lecturing; students at Princeton's Summer School will recall his saltiness and delight in destroying stereotypes of what ministers should be, say, and think. All of this is to acknowledge that Marney's influence was great because of *who he was*, and *how he did what he did*, as much as because of the creativity of his written word. His personality—fresh and spontaneous to his friends, abrasive and unpolished to his critics—was part and parcel of his style as a preacher and his thought as a theologian.

As we attempt to see Marney in the context of his times, it is well to recall the political, cultural, and social issues of America from 1940-78. Like all preachers of the Word, Marney sought to understand and respond to the changing *Zeitgeist*. He sensed the inevitability of change, the need for new symbols and words, the importance of new structures and institutions, and the dramatic impact which science, technology, and the social sciences have had on modern patterns of thought. He knew that the instinctive reaction to change is to look backwards and tried to counter that tendency with every congregation that he served. He understood the habits and patterns of religious commitments from the perspective of cultural anthropology, and knew that many theological appeals to "tradition" were, sociologically speaking, attempts to preserve the folkways. He responded comfortably to the leading theological minds of the times: the Niebuhrs, Tillich, Whitehead, Teilhard, and Barth, but incorporated their work into his own preaching and writing only insofar as they helped him to understand persons. Marney, after he finished his doctoral studies in 1946, never again pursued theology as a formal academic discipline. For him all theological inquiry was a means to a higher end: to understand the complexities of the person, and to gain some hint, however slight, of the purpose of the human pilgrimage. Marney agreed with Aquinas that "the slenderest knowledge that may be obtained of the highest things is more desirable than the most certain knowledge obtained of lesser things." Any thinkers who could help Marney in that quest, be they scientists, novelists, social scientists, poets, philosophers, playwrights or psychologists —he turned to gladly. That basic instinct was what made Marney a *pastoral* theologian — and finally, a Christian humanist. It seemed to Marney that many theologians (not the great ones) and many *followers* of distinguished theologians fail to get their priorities straight about the relationship of theology to personhood.

Marney and the Southern Baptists

Marney's relationship with the Southern Baptist Convention has been a sub-theme throughout the book and now needs to be reviewed more directly. In the Dickson Lectures of 1974, Marney recalled how impressed he was in 1940 when one of his favorite teachers at Southern Baptist Seminary, Dr. Sydnor Stealey, articulated the "five great principles" of the Baptist understanding of the Church. Marney confessed that he was so awed that he thought they would stand forever! They were:

(1) The competency of the individual to deal with God.

(2) The autonomy of the local church.

(3) The sufficiency of the Scriptures.

(4) The separation of Church and State.

(5) The baptism of believers only, and by immersion.[1]

But, Marney noted, all our authorities have wax noses — and each of these principles has been so distorted by history and culture that as now advocated they stand for lies or half-truths. Principle (1) has been taken in the sense that "every tub should have its own bottom" and has thus virtually destroyed the notion of creative fellowship in the church. Principle (2) has been so emphasized that Baptists can no longer fathom the Universal Church of God. Principle (3) has been clung to so avidly that Baptists are almost oblivious to two thousand years of the

---

[1]*Loc cit.,* pp. 38-9.

Church's memory of Jesus Christ. Principle (4) has been so distorted that Baptists have lost the ability to see the intertwining of the concepts of "Secular," "Holy," "World," "Creation," and "Redemption." Principle (5) has caused Baptists to ignore the deeper significance of *initiation* (from birth to death) into the fellowship of Christ Jesus.

Instead of being "Pilgrims," lamented Marney, Baptists have become "tribesmen."[2] What Baptists have missed in their literalistic affirmation of these five principles is the depth of personhood, the creativity of the Living Word, the enrichment made possible by a Pluralistic Freedom, and the broader Domain of the Spirit. In all fairness it must be acknowledged that the criticisms which Marney directed at the Baptists are applicable to other streams of Protestant Christianity as well, but he felt they were particularly relevant to the distortions of faith found within Southern Baptist ranks.

We noted in Chapter II how Marney began his ministry thinking of himself as a "progressive" Baptist, and how as he moved to Austin he wanted to be a force for reform within the Southern Baptist Convention. That desire faded as Marney came to see that all denominations suffer from structural problems and cultural lag, and in fact may be unreformable. If that insight tempered Marney's criticisms of the Baptists, it also dispelled any illusions he had that other denominations were much better. It was in that context that Marney told one of his famous stories about why he remained a Baptist:

> Everywhere I go people ask me why I remain a Baptist. Being a Baptist is like being in a dark, slimy well: it's cold, clammy, uncomfortable and filled with lots of creepy things. For years I tried to climb out, but it was hard: the walls were slippery, I was half-blind, and there were impediments everywhere. Finally, however, I got to the top. I looked around at last to see what the world was like in other denominations. After I had a good look—I just dropped back into the well.[3]

A more determinative point was reached, however, when Marney came to realize that the divisions within the human family are not basically denominational at all, but are the more deeply entrenched

---

[2]*Ibid.,* p. 39.

[3]This story comes from the "oral tradition." It was told to me practically verbatim by two sources, one from Texas and one from South Carolina.

myths of class, race, sex, region, and nationality. It is not surprising therefore that in the last two decades of his life one of Marney's persistent themes was that all serious Christians need to get "beyond the denominations." In Marney's final mode as a Christian-oriented humanist, he wanted to be an interpreter above the pettiness of denominationalism, much as a politician aspires to be a statesman. (It is worth noting that this is only possible when one is no longer required to run for reelection.)

In sum, Marney's history with the Southern Baptists was not a happy one. His public attacks on the denomination came too close to the bone to be turned away without wrath. For many traditional Baptist leaders, Marney was a turncoat—one who should be ignored, repudiated, or pointed out as an example of what "modernism" could do to a person. Marney, standing in a different stream of American intellectual life, knew the toll that Southern Baptist parochialism took on its gifted sons and daughters:

> . . .I can name more than forty men, who represent more than two centuries of graduate study in Europe's best universities, who hold no longer any connection whatever, except nostalgic memory, with the institutions that sired, hired and fired them. Every seminary and graduate school I know in the North and East has its refugees from among the Baptists in the South. This is our best and *only* contribution to the world-church.[4]

Finally the tension with the tradition that birthed him became greater than Marney could sustain. He retained his close friendship with Baptist intellectuals and progressive pastors, and was a welcome guest speaker at Baptist colleges, universities, and seminaries; but emotionally he withdrew from the denomination. In 1974, as he looked back over his years in the ministry, he observed:

> I sum up the whole of my wasted years in a restricted religious group from which I long ago withdrew, for we were not of a kind, by saying: "The only relief from our poor appeal is a proper worship that does not turn *credo* (I believe) into *creed* (the thing believed)."[5]

Anyone who knows the Southern Baptist Convention knows that

---

[4]*Priests to Each Other,* p. 116.

[5]*Ibid.,* p. 81.

it is not monolithic. A number of its scholars are in the main ranks of scholarship in various fields, and creative, prophetic preaching is heard from a number of its pulpits. Marney, because of his style and visibility, was a lightning rod to draw the ire of traditionalists, but he was not alone in his critique of the denomination. Most of the other critics, however, were not as prominent as Marney was nor did they have the professional alternatives that he had. In his day, Marney symbolized an alternative way to a number of friends and young ministers, and his files have many letters expressing appreciation to him for his courage. It is a well-known fact among theologians, clergy, and seminary students that no denomination honors its prophets.

Marney and His Ministerial Audiences

We noted in Chapter IV that Marney had reservations about the future role of ordained clergy, and often spoke harshly about the cowardice, incompetency, and ineffectiveness of the clergy in modern society. The paradox is that year in and year out, state by state across the South and in other areas of the country, ministers turned out to hear Marney. Program planners knew that his presence on a platform would spark attendance, debate, and lively engagement with other conference issues. Why was this the case? Why didn't Marney's sharp words alienate his audiences? The answer, I think, is that in ministerial circles Marney had an earned respect. He had been there. He knew the problems, fears, and temptations of the professional minister from the inside out. He spoke to them not as "you" but as "us"—himself included. And he cared for individuals.

Whatever may be the shortcomings of ministers, it has been my own experience that when they gather together in conclave, two characteristics are present: humor and a distinct capacity to detect phoniness. Most ministers have a critical nose for academic theologians who theorize eloquently but never hit the trenches, and they have an instinctive dislike for "Princes of the Pulpit" who are supercilious, sanctimonious, pompous, or egocentric. Such persons may impress some sycophantic laypeople but they hardly make a dent on their fellow clergy. In such ministerial gatherings, by contrast, Marney came as a *mensch*—a tough, grizzled, unpretentious, earthy man, who could share in their humor, pain, and struggles. Even as he was critical he tried to be constructive. Many a minister who first heard Marney at a conference of some kind eventually came to the Interpreter's House. He counseled with many who left the ministry, encouraged many to stay, and helped countless others regroup personally or relocate.

Marney was to many ministers an illuminating link to the world of academic theology. He helped them understand and utilize concepts which would otherwise have lain fallow in rocky soil. He gave them ideas for reading and models for communication. For all of his criticisms, the world of the ministry was his world, too—and his ministerial audiences knew it.

Did Marney Have a Theological Blind Side?

A good bit of attention was devoted in Chapter III to Marney's intellectual roots: Luther, Freud, Macneile Dixon, John Oman, Rauschenbusch, Fosdick, the Niebuhrs, and Tillich loomed large in his formative years; and as we noted in Chapter IV, at a later time he turned more to Whitehead, Teilhard, Polanyi, and humanistic psychologists. The question of a theological "blind side" is essentially the question of whether a thinker is so committed to one way of understanding the Christian tradition that he never takes seriously other theological alternatives. I can recall the sense of revelation which came to me in the course of my studies on Tillich when—after spending years tracing the roots of and influences on Tillich's thought—I began to think dialectically about those thinkers whom Tillich apparently never read and the perspectives on the Christian tradition which made no impact on him at all. The existence of a "blind side" is difficult to determine since a thinker may well consider other viewpoints and reject them for reasons which are not articulated, but the *via negativa* method of analysis is a valuable way of clarifying the place of any thinker on a broader theological spectrum. A careful assessment reveals that Marney read selectively, and it is both interesting and surprising to note those whom he does *not* quote.

Calvin and the Calvinist heritage, for example, are conspicuously absent from the Marney corpus. Likewise, through most of his career Marney was unenamored of Karl Barth, both because of Barth's Calvinistic orientation and because of his verbosity. (Once when trying to verify something in Barth's writings Marney offered a tentative opinion, but allowed that he might be wrong since he "had only checked four thousand pages."[6]) On the whole, however, Marney felt that Calvin and his successors were much too adamant in their claims to know God; Calvinists, like biblical fundamentalists, tend to speak of knowledge when they should speak of "faith" or "wonder." Marney

---

[6]*The Coming Faith*, p. 100.

was also apprehensive about the potential for militancy or religious fanaticism that is implicit within a Calvinist view. He sympathized with Oliver Cromwell's famous assertion that he "would rather fight all the armies of France than ten Scottish Presbyterians who think they are doing the will of God." Although Marney had cordial relationships with the major Presbyterian denominations in America, he had difficulty in appreciating the positive side of Calvinistic theology.

Wesley and leading interpreters of Methodism are likewise seldom cited in Marney's writings or sermons, probably because he was dubious about any perspective on the Christian life which spoke of "sanctification" or "edification.". Marney's own debt to Freud clearly led him to feel that the Wesleyan tradition was founded on an inadequate anthropology. That, in turn, seemed to keep Marney from appreciating the heartiness and evangelistic fervor which shaped so much of Methodism. Marney's engagement with Luther, rather, seems to have been so strong that he never seriously wrestled with Wesley.

In a world that has become increasingly indebted to Marx and the Marxian critique of economic and political structures, it is surprising that Marney practically never quoted Marx (save for his chapter on "Materialism" in *The Structures of Prejudice*) nor did he show any scholarly interest in Marxist studies in ideology. Similarly Marney drew on no Roman Catholic thinkers other than Teilhard de Chardin, even in the ecumenical era ushered in by Vatican II. He never cited Martin Luther King's writings, nor did he apparently think it necessary to assess, or respond to, any of the theological critiques developed by Black theology. (He may well have felt that he was leveling those same charges against White churches long before the Black theologians came on the scene!) The Women's Movement in theology passed him by, as apparently did the third world voices who began to reach Western ears in the early 1970's: Bonino, Gutierrez, Segundo, Boff, and others. He did not appear to draw on the work of leading contemporary Protestant ethicists (such as James Gustafson, Stanley Hauerwas, and Roger Shinn) or other American theologians who shared many of his interests vis-a-vis theory and practice (Robert McAfee Brown and Harvey Cox, for example). He had little interest in the contribution of Jürgen Moltmann and contemporary German theology; the one reference I located concerning Pannenberg was quite negative, concluding that Pannenberg was attempting to substitute "knowledge" for "faith." (That criticism, of course, is not unique with Marney.)

Our concern about these lacunae must be tempered, however, with the realization that Marney never pursued theological study as an end in itself, nor was he interested in theological interactions within the history of ideas. The insistence on "balance" or "perspective" in academic theology is therefore not really applicable to him. Clearly he regarded many theologians as too academic; others he probably judged to have concerns which were not the concerns of his audiences. It must be pointed out, however, that Marney's failure to acknowledge certain thinkers does not mean that he did not incorporate their concerns in his own thought and language. With most southern audiences, for example, it is more persuasive to speak of the myths that bind us than to lecture about Marx's theory of ideology. It is more effective to speak of the limitations of regionalism or ethnicity than to discourse on the sociology of knowledge. When one addresses Southern white audiences on the race problem, it is undoubtedly more effective to speak prophetically and confessionally as a white man than it is to pepper one's manuscript with quotations from Martin Luther King or James Cone. There was wisdom in Marney's method.

The one mythic structure which Marney never consciously escaped, as far as I can ascertain, is that of *maleness*. He was unrepentant in his use of the generic term "Man," in his frequent appeals for our "Common Manhood," and in his utilization of masculine terminology for God. For all of his interests in the grammar of faith, he seemed oblivious to the issues raised by feminist theologians about the problem of God-language and the patriarchal structure of the faith. His clever and generally delightful view of Heaven, reprinted as an Epilogue to this book, betrays an inherent sexism guaranteed to offend even mild-mannered feminists. Even when we acknowledge that he wrote that piece in 1963, it is a troubling deficiency in so sensitive a human being.

The question of Marney's theological blind side cannot be left without some consideration of his attitude towards more conservative understandings of the Christian tradition. After breaking out of a conservative background of his own while a seminary student, he had difficulty in seeing the strengths which can sometimes be found among people of that persuasion. Perhaps the hurts in him were too deep to be healed, but even in his last decade as he spoke more about the heart and the mind, he seemed unable to muster much charity towards Christian conservatives. None of his lectures or notes which I found indicated that he saw much difference between the various shades of biblical conservatives. He never quoted from the more reputable conservative theologians—Carl F.H. Henry, Donald Dayton, Jim Wallis—nor took seriously the stirrings within the evangelical ranks to articulate a socially-conscious faith. When invited to participate in a dialogue with conservatives in the last year of his life, he stunned some of the participants with his acrimony and repudiation of their assumptions. Marney said on several occasions that he could deal with conservatives who have some grace and humor, but he found few, and he continued to harbor deep resentments about their exclusivism and theological certainty. The more militant the evangelical, the more Marney was persuaded that this was an enemy of universal humanism. Whether this constitutes a "blind side" is arguable, but minimally we must acknowledge that there was a part of the Christian family to whom Marney could not relate and to whom he could not be a bearer of grace.

This analysis of Marney's place in the broader theological spectrum illumines that Marney was an eclectic thinker: he drew heavily from some sources, ignored others, found his own language for old ideas, bore and bared some hurts, and, like all thinkers, found some things easier to talk about than to implement in his own life. He had several "blind sides," but was remarkably alert to theological issues and participated responsibly in the broader ranges of theological discussion. Various critics may wish that he had paid more attention to their special interests or mentors, but Marney was in no way a parochial or one-sided theologian.

Marney's Legacy to the Future

Will—or should—a future generation read Marney when his ideas are no longer seen through the glow of his own colorful personality? That question forces us to look at the intrinsic value of his writings. Persons of the 1980's may not even have a choice. Only two of his books—*The Recovery of the Person* (recently reissued as a paperback by Abingdon) and *Priests to Each Other*—are still in print, although it is possible that one or two of his other works might be reissued. It seems clear that he will not be remembered by academic theologians or technical scholars, but he never considered them his audience anyway. Will Marney make a distinctive contribution to ministers and laypeople in a new decade?

As a church theologian, it is uncertain how much of Marney's work will impact on future generations. Marney himself knew that all theological writing is historically conditioned and once noted that except for a few theological "giants," only a handful of earlier writers are still worth reading. He knew that the theological solutions of yesterday cannot be re-heated for today's problems. Some of Marney's *emphases*, however, may well be center stage for the theological agenda of the future. Harry Emerson Fosdick, in his insightful autobiography entitled *The Living of These Days*, observed in passing that he thought every minister only had two or three "good fights" in him during a lifetime, and that a minister should therefore choose very carefully the issues for which he was prepared to go to the mat. These wise words, reminding us that everyone has limitations of strength and vitality, help us to see that even creative theologians are limited in what they can contribute uniquely to the climate of Christian thought in a lifetime. Setting Marney against the broader theological and ecclesiastical backdrop of his times, three major themes emerge:

a. *The Centrality of the Person.* Marney reminds us that unless theology considers the person and is oriented to the complexities of the human pilgrimage, it is ultimately of value only for archivists and to fill dusty library shelves. His creativity in utilizing the thought of the philosophers and theologians of Personal Being—and of interpreting that in a pastoral context—is surely a vital example for both theologians and ministers in the next decade.

b. *The Vision of a Good Society.* Marney's late realization that humanity itself is endangered, and that there can be no good community without some dedication to a Whole greater than the individual, is—if not unique to Marney—clearly a theme for the future. The task of myth-breaking, of becoming liberated from the structures which distort and bind us, is consistent with what other leading thinkers are beginning to affirm as the major priority of the next decade. (See, for example, Robert McAfee Brown's *Theology in a New Key* [Westminster Press, 1978].) Marney is an excellent model of how to communicate that concern to laypeople both inside and outside the churches.

c. *A Forward Looking Church.* Marney knew that all forms pass away, and that a vital Church of tomorrow may well look very different from what we have known. Throughout his ministry he advocated a Church that was unafraid; he believed in a Church that could get its priorities straight. Marney's writings assuage guilt feelings in those who are influenced by the Christian tradition and want to work towards a better society, but who are uninterested in current patterns and forms of Church life. Marney's emphasis on the concept of vocation can revitalize the laity and open the clergy to new patterns of ministry.

In and through these emphases, Marney is surely a theologian who can be read with profit in the next decade. It is sad that his best medium of communication, the spoken word, cannot be a major part of his ongoing influence. His sermons from his last decade which are in manuscript form lack the tightness and clarity of the sermons of Fosdick or Buttrick, and betray how much of his effectiveness from the pulpit was related to his charisma and personality. Those who possess tapes of his sermons or lectures will replay them on occasion, not so much because they can offer new ideas, but because they will be reminders of his distinctive personality and inspiration. If Marney's unique way of addressing problems is not emulated, at least those who return to his theological writings will find a rich example as to *how* problems can be addressed from the boundary between pastoral care and theological reflection.

As a churchman, Marney leaves a different legacy. He will be remembered by troubled Baptists, searching Methodists, ecumenical Presbyterians, progressive Disciples, Teilhard-type Catholics, and some Reform Jews. He will be remembered by those who are troubled by denominationalism, by those who suspect that what passes for "Christianity" in middle America is too uncritically tied to middle-class values, and by those who resent moralisms replacing social conscience in religious communities. He will appeal to a group which moves easily into the secular structures of society with their strengths and talents without worrying whether or not they are conventionally religious. Humanists of many stripes will find in him a model of what an "outward-looking" Christianity might be. Those committed to new forms of Church life will find him a prophetic figure.

As a person, however, Marney's impact will obviously live on in the oral tradition. Even those who only knew him through others will be heartened by his courage, his candor, his humanity, his compassion and his de-bunking of religious mythologies. Perhaps the best tribute which can be paid to him is to note that he lived with a consistency in his life and thought, and with an integrity to his roots and to his covenants. This is the witness which, over many centuries, has made a small handful of Christian leaders men—and women—for all seasons.

Hail and Farewell!

This salutation, used by Marney in the first of his 1974 Dickson Lectures, is an appropriate rubric as we bring this study of Marney to a close. If Marney would be amused at this endeavor to trace his pilgrimage and to give some perspective on his eclectic and evolving writings, I hope he would at the same time be modestly pleased by a tribute from one who felt only the broader ripples of his influence. Marney, I suspect, would make no claims himself for his ongoing influence. He would probably say he did the best he could, with what he had, where he was, given the complexities of his own being and his struggle for faith.

Marney, as we have noted several times throughout this study, loved music in both classical and popular forms. He often said that theological mysteries could best be understood through musical imagery. As a tribute to his classical interests, it was appropriate that the selections "And the Glory of the Lord" and "The Trumpet Shall Sound," both from Handel's *Messiah,* were played at the Memorial Service held for him at Myers Park Baptist Church. In a lighter vein, and perhaps more consistent with his Tennessee roots, Marney liked the trombone, march music, and music that stirred the soul. If we can end this study on a celestial note, Karl Barth said on several occasions that the only thing he felt sure would be in heaven was the music of Mozart. We might envision Marney, upon arrival in Heaven, startling Barth's rhapsodic contemplation by leading a troupe of fellow viators playing "Seventy-Six Trombones."

EPILOGUE: MARNEY'S VISION OF HEAVEN

"Such a sleep they sleep, those men I loved."

—Source unknown, a favorite quotation of Marney's.

The final word in this volume deserves to be Marney's own. The following description of the "heaven of his fancy" captures much of the humor and earthiness of this Southern Sojourner. It was written for *The Recovery of the Person* in 1963:

"The heaven of my fancy would contain, I fear, no pietists, no scientists, no mathematicians, nor any other kind of fundamentalist. It would consist, in the main, of a small coterie of agreeable theologians, not too smart for me, who generally are in agreement with me, and who speak English. There would be few, if any, Yankees, for I find them very provincial; no Democrats or Republicans, for they all sound alike; but a few stout atheists for spite and for everyone else's amusement.

As for women, there would be a few: my own wife and daughters, not from duty, but because I happen to like them; the wives of some of my friends, but not all; a few enjoyable female seekers and theologians whom I have found to be able to disagree like gentlemen, and then, a few for decoration. My mother, of course, if she really liked it and decided to stay, and a few of the children whose love has made the pastorate worth the trouble.

My heaven would include my father, because he has never in all his life presumed on the Almighty just because of his faith. It would include almost no theological students, for they are arrogant and know far too much for my heaven. There would be a few rascals, one *carajan* mechanic I know to fix things where he wouldn't charge for it, a deacon or two, most of the men I have worked with, a hunting buddy, a few animals I have loved, some trees and a river, mountains and a moon, and frost and fall and summer. There would be some odors, some memories, and a few unanswered questions to push around; no games, no puzzles, no charts, no calendars, no engagement pads. I would include a few books and one or two writers I have read a lot; a Catholic priest I knew in Korea, an old uncle who would be so surprised he would be fun to watch; no germs, no debts, no money, no Brussels sprouts, no elections, no high-church Anglicans, no professional pastors, no denominational experts, no finance campaigns, and no Saturday evenings without a sermon ready.

No linguists, no faddists, no experts on anything, but I would need a good flutist, a good organist, and one real tenor. I'm not sure about real Presbyterians or Disciples, though many are an agreeable lot, and one or two salesmen because of all they have to put up with and for Willie Loman's sake.

I would take a boyhood friend or two; a good saddle, a good knife and a hearty appetite, but no pills, tranquilizers, hair curlers, tweezers, or stiff petticoats." (pp. 131-133).

need sermons by George
Buttrick → Riverside
Church

APPENDIX I

THREE TRIBUTES TO MARNEY
AS THEOLOGIAN AND CHURCHMAN

1. From Donald W. Shriver, Jr., President, Union Theological Seminary, New York City:

As I came to know Marney, he impressed me in three ways: First was his massive eloquence. He came to Harvard once while I was a graduate student in the early sixties, and I remember that he *stretched* the use of the English Language in the pulpit, forced words into the service of Gospel-preaching as no one on that campus, besides George Buttrick, had been able to do. That he did this in a southern accent did all the more, in that church, to deliver it from Yankee provincialism! Second was his deep, inner prophetic security that enabled him to demonstrate, in the mid-sixties, the connection between the role of the prophet and the role of the pastor in a local southern congregation. Those were difficult days for young pastors in the South who knew that the Bible was on the side of human equality, that racism was overdue its biblical critique, but that this culture made it difficult to talk of "love" and "justice" in the same sermon or pastoral conversation. Marney made credible the idea that you might be called to love people *out of* their racial prejudice. Finally, he drove home this pastoral-prophetic credibility to me as a person and a friend during the last years of his life. In the several conversations of these years he always managed to fortify my courage for continuing to do exactly what I had put my hand to doing. Whether at North Carolina State University, or Emory, or Union Seminary in New York, he always tempered the natural self-doubt that many a Protestant among us nourished in our heart of hearts. "You know what you are doing, God knows what you are doing, so stop worrying!" he seemed to say. It is a privilege to know people who believe in you more than you are apt to believe in yourself. Marney was one of the country's great pastors to pastors. As such, he was one of the great educators of the educators of our calling.

2. From James I. McCord, President, Princeton Theological Seminary:

Carlyle Marney was *sui generis*. He had the body of a wrestler and the soul of a poet. The first thing of his that I read was a series of sermons on Dostoievski, produced when he was a young pastor in Austin, Texas. His understanding of the Russian novelist's passionate concern for freedom was matched by his own existential awareness of modern man's bondage to culture and to the idols of the marketplace. We asked him to join the Austin Seminary faculty, with responsibility for a course in preaching, but soon discovered our mistake. Marney was a great preacher, but no one could imitate him. He used words as building blocks, piling one upon the other, and the effect was powerful. His poor students tripped and fell time and again as they tried to follow the master wordsman. Marney shifted to the field of social ethics and the results were electrifying. His concern for the poor, the exploited, the Chicano, and the black, was contagious, and a new dimension was added to the ministry of those who sat at his feet.

At Princeton the results were the same. Although we could not induce him to join our faculty on a permanent basis, he was present for some important occasion each year for nearly two decades, lecturing, preaching, counseling, and encouraging.

What was Marney's secret? He was a free man, one who stood free in the Gospel. It was this freedom, plus his remarkable gifts and wide-range reading, that gave him his extraordinary power as a minister of the Gospel of Jesus Christ. To me Marney incarnated the best in the Free Church tradition.

"Vast intellectual
Capital"

3. From Thomas A. Langford, Dean, Duke Divinity School:

There are many testimonies to Marney's influence. His preaching, the congregations he served, the friends he retained, the students he taught, and the minister whose ministry he saved. Interpreter's House was a place for respite, for renewal, for conviction, and for celebration. Interpreter's House was Marney. He led some people apart only to return them with new strength to their homes and churches.

For six years Marney had been teaching with us at Duke. The coming of Marney to Duke was a reunion with many friends. He used to say that some of his closest friends were on the faculty of the Divinity School. I got to know Marney personally only seven years ago. I was newly appointed to the deanship and was spending the summer in the mountains. Marney called and then came to talk. We discussed programs and plans and future directions, but mostly we came to know one another. As time has passed we have had opportunity to share a common love of the mountains and the school, to share food and conversation. The time together has been good.

As Ann Marie and I forded the creek of Wolf Pen Mountain the afternoon of his death and parked in front of the apple house I knew that the turn of time had brought a major change. Marney was gone. A witness had been completed and that to which he had contributed must now be carried by others in their own distinctive ways. Marney would not want mimics but he would want full-bodied, independent, courageous, sensitive, robust ministers. He opened a way; he helped some along this path; he has left us the mountain. (Adapted from a longer statement in *Duke Divinity School in Ministry*, August, 1978, p. 4. Reprinted by permission.)

Appendix II

Books on Marney's desk at the time of his death

William Strunk, Jr. and E. B. White, *The Elements of Style*
John Bunyan, *Pilgrim's Progress* (two different editions)
Franz Fanon, *The Wretched of the Earth*
John Doberstein, *The Minister's Prayer Book*
Robert W. Bailey, *The Minister and Grief*
Dante, *Divine Comedy*
Augustine, *Letters*
The Greek New Testament

Appendix III

Marney's List of His Eleven Most Influential Books

Augustine, *Confessions*
Otto, *The Idea of the Holy*
Dixon, *The Human Situation*
Temple, *Nature, Man and God*
Dostoievski, *The Brothers Karamazov*
Unamuno, *The Tragic Sense of Life*
Harnack, *What Is Christianity?*
Berdyaev, *The Destiny of Man*
Brunner, *The Divine Imperative* and *The Divine-Human Encounter*
Kierkegaard, *Sickness unto Death*
Baillie, *Our Knowledge of God*

INDEX